Blüten

Kerstin Theobald

à la Carte

Tischdekorationen für viele Anlässe
Stunning table decorations

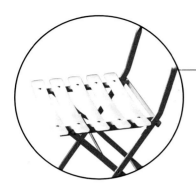

Vorwort

Gemeinsames Essen und Trinken ist ein wesentlicher Bestandteil unserer Kultur und gilt als Ausdruck unseres Lebensstils. Zusammen mit Freunden, Verwandten, Kollegen oder Geschäftspartnern zu feiern, ist beliebt wie nie zuvor. Dabei soll die Feier nicht nur in kulinarischer Hinsicht zum Highlight werden. Mit allen Sinnen genießen lautet das aktuelle Motto. An vorderster Stelle steht dabei die Tischdekoration. Denn schließlich isst das Auge mit, und an einem schön gedeckten und mit Blumen dekorierten Tisch schmeckt es gleich nochmal so gut.

Vor allem, wenn es um die Dekoration größerer Feste, Parties und Events geht, wenden sich die meisten Gastgeber und Veranstalter gerne an Sie als Florist und vertrauen auf Ihre fachliche Kompetenz. In diesem Buch finden Sie daher jede Menge begeisternde Gestaltungsideen für ganz unterschiedliche Anlässe. Denn ob im privaten Rahmen ein 50ster Geburtstag gefeiert wird oder auf repräsentative Weise ein Firmenjubiläum begangen werden soll, macht bei der Dekoration einen großen Unterschied. Dabei sind nicht immer aufwändige und komplizierte Blumenarrangements die größten Hingucker. Oft ist es einfach die originelle Idee, die sich mit wenigen Handgriffen verwirklichen lässt und dabei den größten Effekt erzielt. Alle unsere Vorschläge lassen sich je nach Gästezahl und Größe der Tische beliebig erweitern. Zu jeder Grundgestaltung gibt es ein bis zwei Varianten, die besonders unkompliziert zu erstellen sind, sowie zahlreiche Schritt-für-Schritt-Anleitungen.

Wir hoffen, Ihnen damit einen anschaulichen und praxisnahen Ratgeber an die Hand zu geben, aus dem Sie bei der täglichen Arbeit immer wieder schöpfen können.

Wir wünschen Ihnen viel Erfolg bei der Umsetzung und Weiterentwicklung der Ideen.

Ihre Kerstin Theobald
und das 'profil floral'-Team

Eating and drinking in the company of others is an essential component of our culture and is generally viewed as an expression of our lifestyles. Celebrating with friends, relatives, colleagues or business partners has become more popular than ever before. And the food is no longer the only highlight at such parties. Today's demanding guests want to enjoy such an event with all their senses. And at the top of the list of "must-haves" are sumptuous floral table decorations. After all, today's guests also want something to feast their eyes on, and at a table decorated with delectable flowers everything is bound to taste twice as good.

Especially in the case of decorations for larger parties and events, most hostesses or organisers prefer to leave the floral arrangements in the capable hands of a professional florist. Therefore, in this book you will find lots of inspiring creative ideas for all kinds of occasions. Because whether it's a 50th birthday being toasted in private surroundings or a company function organised in a more prestigious style, the floral decorations can make a really big difference. And arrangements do not have to be huge, overwhelming and complicated bouquets to be eye-catching and appropriate. Quite often the designs with the most stunning impact stem from a simple, original idea that can be implemented with just a few twists of the wrist. All of our ideas can be streamlined to almost any size of table and number of guests. We have included two variations on every theme, all very easy to construct, as well as numerous step-by-step how-to instructions to help you duplicate them.

We hope this book will provide you with an illustrative and practice-oriented manual that will often lend a helping hand in your daily work with flowers.

We wish you much success in trying out our ideas and improving on them with ideas of your own.

Kerstin Theobald
and the 'profil floral' team

Feste im Freien

Feste unter freiem Himmel gehören zu den schönsten Ereignissen des Sommers. Zum einen, weil sie das Unbeschwerte und die Heiterkeit der Jahreszeit widerspiegeln. Zum anderen, weil unsere nördlichen Breitengrade sie nur an wenigen Tagen im Jahr ermöglichen. Dies macht zwar den ganz besonderen und einzigartigen Charme dieser Feste aus. Damit verbunden sind aber auch spezielle Anforderungen, denen man bei der Planung eines solchen Events gerecht werden muss. So darf die Dekoration nicht zu aufwändig ausfallen. Sie sollte leichtem Wind und einzelnen Regentropfen standhalten. Gegebenenfalls muss sie sich sogar auf die Schnelle und ohne großen Aufwand komplett ins Trockene transportieren lassen. Dies schmälert jedoch keinesfalls die Attraktivität einer solchen Dekoration. Im Gegenteil: Gerade darin liegt der besondere Reiz der Gestaltung.

Among the most enjoyable experiences of summer is having parties out-of-doors. For one, because they reflect the carefree and cheerful feeling of this time of year. For another, due to our northern latitudes, they are only possible on very few days each year. This is what makes the charm of such get-togethers so special and unique. However, at the same time they are also subject to special requirements, which must always be taken into consideration when planning such events. For example the decorations should be kept relatively simple. They may have to withstand a light breeze and maybe a few drops of rain. Worse come to worst, they might even have to be whisked inside, so they should also be easy to transport. However, these factors needn't reduce the attractiveness of such decorations. Au contraire: that's where the special charm of these creations lies.

celebrating outside

summer celebration – garden party – outdoor fete

Bottleparty
auf unkomplizierte Art
bottle party
the uncomplicated way

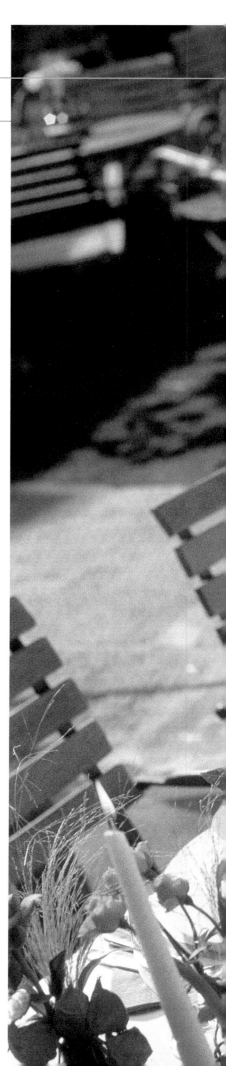

Flaschen anstelle von Vasen. Unkompliziert und zwanglos soll es bei einem Fest im Freien zugehen. Zerbrechliche Gefäße aus feinem Glas haben dabei nichts verloren. Zu groß wäre die Gefahr, dass sie durch Transport oder Wind eventuell Schaden nehmen könnten. Am besten greift man daher auf schlichte Gefäße aus dem täglichen Gebrauch zurück. Soll die Dekoration rustikal wirken, eignen sich Bierflaschen mit Bügelverschluss, wer es optisch etwas verspielter und leichter bevorzugt, verwendet kleine Limo- oder Camparifläschchen. In jedem Fall werden sämtliche Flaschen von ihren Etiketten befreit und je nach Geschmack mit floristischen Accessoires aufgepeppt. Eine spätsommerliche Blütenmischung in sonnigen Farben ist die ideale Füllung für die zweckentfremdeten Flaschen.

Bottles for vases. Outdoor parties should be uncomplicated and informal. Therefore, fragile containers of delicate glass are better off not being invited. The danger of them being chipped or broken during transport or knocked over by the wind is too great. So why not reinvent some simple vessels from everyday use? Especially suitable for creating a rustic look are beer bottles with old-fashioned fliptop closures, or if you want a lighter and more playful effect, use small soda or Campari bottles. In any case, the labels are first removed from all the bottles and the new vases are then jazzed up with floral accessories — depending on personal taste. A late-summer mix of flowers in sunny colours will make an ideal filling for bottles in new-found roles.

Einzelne Flaschen mit Accessoires. Besonders flexibel gestaltet sich die Dekorationsidee, wenn man die einzelnen Bierflaschen in kleinen Gruppen auf der Tafel platziert. Dabei werden die Flaschen mit unterschiedlichen, selbst hergestellten Accessoires, wie kleinen Kränzen, Filzringen oder Bandumwicklungen, verziert. Der Vorteil dieser Variante: Die Idee lässt sich je nach Gästezahl beliebig fortführen.

Individual bottles with accessories. This deco idea is particularly flexible if the beer bottles are placed in small groups on the table. Each bottle is adorned with different handmade accessories, such as tiny wreaths, felt rings or bands of ribbon. The advantage of this variation: depending on the number of guests invited, this creative idea can be carried on almost infinitely.

Ob als breite Ummantelung mit aufgeklebtem Rebenbinde-garnkranz oder als schmaler Ring um die Flasche gelegt: Das robuste Material Filz eignet sich gut für eine trendige Akzentuie-rung der Bierflaschendekoration.

Whether as a wide encirclement with a glued-on wreath of florists' twine or a narrow ring placed around the bottle: felt is a sturdy material that is well-suited for a trendy accentuation in the beer bottle theme.

Orangefarbene Accessoires ste-hen im leuchtenden Kontrast zu den braunen Flaschen und passen perfekt zur Blütenmi-schung. *Physalis*-Früchte werden auf Draht gefädelt, zum Kranz geformt, mit herabhängenden Bändchen verziert und einfach um den Flaschenhals gelegt.

Orange-coloured accessories stand in brilliant contrast to the brown bottles and also make a perfect match for the combination of florals. *Physalis* seedpods are strung on a wire, which is then bent into a wreath shape, adorned with a few hanging ribbons and then simply arranged around the neck of the bottle.

Kleine Kränzchen aus *Buxus* sind mit gelbem Band umwickelt und damit an die Flaschen gebunden. Je nach Größe können sie auch direkt um den Flaschenhals gelegt oder aus Gras gewickelt werden.

Tiny wreaths of *Buxus* are encir-cled with yellow ribbon and then attached to the bottles. Depending on size, they can be slung around the neck of the bottle, or wound of grass.

Flaschen im Quartett. Etwas kompakter wirkt diese Dekorationsvariante, die auf einer Vierergruppierung der Flaschen basiert. Sie lässt sich ebenfalls beliebig erweitern oder auch für kleinere Tische reduzieren. Als Basis dienen Spanholzplatten, die auf ein quadratisches Format gesägt und mit wasserfester, oranger Farbe gestrichen sind.

Bottles in a quartet. This deco alternative appears somewhat more compact, based on groupings of four bottles. The design can also be expanded as necessary or reduced for smaller tables. The base is provided by a square of chipboard, cut to size and then given a coat of oil-based orange paint.

Die Flaschen werden jeweils in Vierergruppen mit Rebenbinde-garn zusammengebunden, mit Wasser und Blüten gefüllt und mittig auf den Holzplatten platziert. Wer sicher gehen will, fixiert die Gefäße mit Heißkleber.

The bottles are tied together in groups of four with florists' twine, filled with water and flowers and then placed in the centre of the wooden squares. For added stability the bottles can be secured with hot glue.

Die Flaschen von den Etiketten befreien und jeweils zu viert zusammenbinden. Dafür zunächst mit ein bis zwei Haushaltsgummis fixieren.

Remove the labels from the bottles and tie together in a group of four. To begin with, secure with two household rubber bands.

Anschließend die Flaschengruppe mehrfach mit Rebenbindegarn umwickeln, so dass die Gummi-bänder verdeckt werden. Anfang und Ende miteinander verzwir-beln und unter die Umwicklung schieben.

Then wrap several loops of florists' twine around the quartet, making sure to conceal the elastic bands completely. Twirl the ends of string together and push under the encir-clement.

Ganz im Stil der Flaschen-dekoration lassen sich auch Platzkarten anfertigen. Eine Flasche pro Tisch wird anstelle des alten Etiketts auf farblich passendem Papier mit den Namen der Gäste beschriftet.

Matching place cards in step with the bottle theme can also be done up quickly and easily. One bottle per table is given a bright new label of paper in a matching shade, on which the names of the guests are listed.

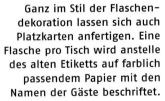

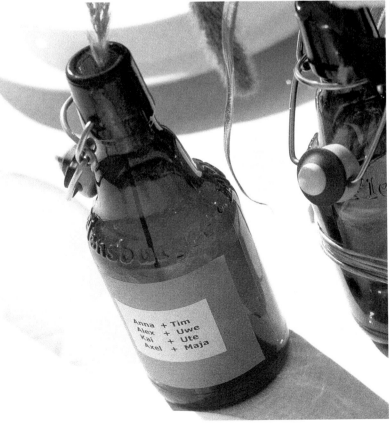

Anna + Tim
Alex + Uwe
Kai + Ute
Axel + Maja

Flaschen als Fries. Traditioneller und dabei dennoch zeitgemäß und spontan wirkt die Bierflaschendekoration, wenn sie als langer Fries in der Mitte des Tisches arrangiert wird. Diese Variante eignet sich besonders für längere Tafeln. Die mit Blüten gefüllten Flaschen werden auf einem langen Holzbrett in doppelter Reihe eng nebeneinander gestellt und evtl. mit Heißkleber fixiert. Über den Tisch gestreute, einzelne *Physalis*-Früchte lockern die Anordnung auf.

Bottles in a frieze. For a more traditional and yet up-to-the-minute beer bottle decoration, arrange them in a long frieze down the centre of the table. This variant is particularly appropriate for longer dining tables. The bottles are filled with water and flowers and then positioned closely together in a double row on a long wooden board. For added stability they can be secured with hot glue. Single *Physalis* seedpods, strewn over the table here and there, loosen up the arrangement.

Die Bierflaschen werden so angeordnet, dass ihre Bügelverschlüsse alle in die gleiche Richtung zeigen. Wichtig: Beim Einstellen der Blüten und Gräser sollte darauf geachtet werden, dass die Dekoration insgesamt nicht zu hoch gerät.

The beer bottles are arranged with their porcelain fliptop closures towards the outside, for maximum impact. Important: when arranging the flowers and grasses in the bottles, take care to keep the assembly below eye level.

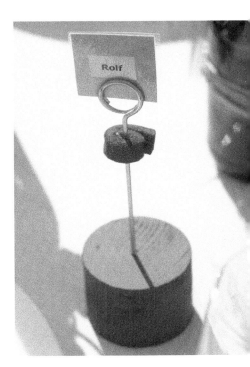

Statt konventioneller Tischkarten verraten kleine *Physalis*-Kränzchen den Gästen, wo sie sitzen. Die Früchte werden dazu auf Draht gefädelt und mit einem beschrifteten Papierschildchen versehen.

Instead of conventional place cards, tiny *Physalis* wreaths tell the guests where they are to sit. To make these, string the seedpods on a stub wire, bend into a ring and top with a paper name tag.

Die Namensschildhalter aus Holzscheiben und mit Hilfe eines Akkubohrers eingesetzten Etikettierstäben sind mehrfach verwendbar. Filzband setzt zusätzliche Akzente, das beschriftete Papier ist lamiert.

For more practical, reusable name cards, the stem of a ready-made cardholder is inserted in the centre of a thick wooden disc, with the help of a cordless drill. Felt supplies additional accents, the name tag is a laminated square of paper.

Schnapsideen

in Regenbogenfarben

bright ideas

in rainbow colours

Blütenmix im Schnapsglas. Schnell gemacht und besonders fröhlich und unbeschwert in ihrer Wirkung ist diese Outdoor-Dekoration mit Schnapsgläsern. Damit nichts zu Bruch gehen kann, kommen Gläser aus durchsichtigem Kunststoff zum Einsatz, die in Supermärkten, Kaufhäusern oder im Lebensmittelgroßhandel erhältlich sind. Die farbliche Wirkung der bunten Blütenmischung wird zusätzlich durch einige Tropfen Aquacolor im Wasser verstärkt. Je bunter die Blütenzusammenstellung, desto fröhlicher die Gesamtwirkung, die große Bandbreite des Sommerflors kann dabei voll ausgeschöpft werden. Ein weiterer Vorteil: Auch bereits weit aufgeblühte Blüten oder solche, deren Stiel evtl. abgeknickt ist, können bei dieser Dekoration problemlos verwendet werden.

Floral mix in schnapps glasses. This outdoor decoration with shot glasses is quick and easy to make and has an especially cheery and carefree look. To prevent anything from getting broken, we have used glasses of clear plastic, which can be bought at supermarkets, department stores or grocery wholesalers. The colourful effect of the bright combination of flowers is further underscored by adding a few drops of watercolour to the water. The more brightly-coloured the florals, the more cheerful the overall impact – and the sky's the limit to the abundance of summer flora that can be used. Another advantage: even flowers in full bloom or those with bent stems can be used in this decoration without any problem.

Blütenmischung im Quadrat. Wenn die Blütengläschen auf quadratischen Holzplatten angeordnet werden, so ist dies nicht nur besonders dekorativ, sondern darüber hinaus auch äußerst praktisch. Die Kunststoffgläser werden mit Heißkleber auf einfarbig gestrichenen Holzplatten fixiert, so kann beim Transport nichts umfallen oder vom Wind weggeblasen werden. Erst vor Ort werden die Gläser mit Wasser und Blüten gefüllt.

Square dance of flowers. If the tiny vases are arranged on square wooden boards, the look is not only particularly decorative but also extremely functional. The clear plastic glasses are hot-glued to a monochrome-painted piece of wood, so that nothing can tip over during transport or if the wind picks up later. The water and flowers are added right on the table.

Die quadratische Grundform der Holzplatten wird auch bei den Tischkartenhaltern wieder aufgegriffen. In einem kleinen eckigen Metallschälchen finden einzelne Blütenblätter Platz. Daran wird das laminierte Namensschildchen mit Hilfe einer selbst geformten Drahtschnecke befestigt.

The square shape of the wooden board is again reflected in the place card holders. In small square metal boxes individual flower petals find their niche. The name tag is attached with the help of a handmade coil of stub wire.

Der Sommer hält eine große Auswahl an Blüten bereit. Geeignet sind vor allem kleinere und kurzstielige Blüten, Blätter und Beeren, die mal einzeln, mal zu mehreren in die mit farbigem Wasser gefüllten Schnapsgläser gesetzt werden.

Summer holds a huge selection of flowers in store. Most suitable are smaller and short-stemmed flowers, foliage and berries, which can be arranged either alone or together in the coloured water in the schnapps glasses.

In Reih' und Glied als Blütenteppich. Ein blühender Tisch-läufer entsteht, wenn die blütengefüllten Schnapsgläschen auf einem langen, mit Acrylfarbe gestrichenen Holzbrett befestigt werden. Für einen üppigen Gesamteindruck sollten es mindestens drei Gläserreihen sein. Je nach Tafellänge können die Bretter dabei nahtlos aneinander gelegt werden.

In rank and file as a floral carpet. A blooming table runner can be created if the schnapps glasses of flowers are attached to a long board painted with a coat of acrylic paint. For greater impact, at least three rows of glasses will be necessary. Depending on the length of the table, several boards can be placed together seamlessly.

Beim Fixieren der Kunststoffgläser mit Heißkleber müssen
die Gläschen akkurat neben-
und hintereinander auf der
Holzplatte befestigt werden.
Andernfalls ginge die grafische
Wirkung des Blütenteppichs
verloren.

When affixing the plastic glasses
with hot glue, be careful to place
them accurately in even rows on
the wooden board. Otherwise the
graphic effect of the floral
carpet will be diminished.

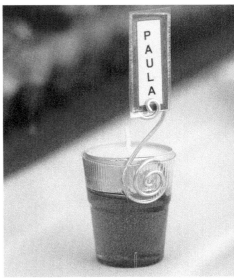

Für den Serviettenschmuck
wird eine schlichte weiße
Serviette gerollt, mit schmalem
pinkfarbenem Band zusammengehalten und mit einer einzelnen, farblich passenden Blüte
einfach darunter geschoben.

For the serviette rings, a plain
white serviette is rolled together,
secured with a pink ribbon and
adorned with a single flower in
a matching shade, tucked inside
the ribbon.

Tischkarte und stimmungsvolle
Beleuchtung zugleich: In die
mit farbigem Wasser gefüllten
Schnapsgläser werden Teelichter
eingeklemmt und die laminierten
Namensschildchen mit selbst
geformten Drahtschnecken
daran befestigt.

Place cards and attractive illumination in one: tea lights are fitted in
the tops of schnapps glasses filled
with coloured water, and the laminated name tags are attached with
handmade coils of stub wire.

Coole Variante mit Metallpodest. Wenn die Dekoration etwas weniger farbig ausfallen und allein durch die Blütenmischung wirken soll, können die Schnapsgläser auch auf Zinkpodesten, anstelle von bunten Holzplatten, befestigt werden. Dafür eignen sich niedrige eckige Zinkwannen, die zweckentfrem- det und umgedreht auf der Tafel platziert werden. Den Blüten kommt damit im wahrsten Sinne des Wortes erhöhte Aufmerksamkeit zu.

Cool customers on metal platforms. If the decoration is to be less colourful in honour of the presentation of the floral mix, the schnapps glasses can also be displayed on zinc platforms instead of brightly- coloured wooden boards. The perfect solution: shallow rectangular zinc troughs are given a new role and placed upside-down on the table. This guarantees the flowers heightened attention – in every sense of the word.

Die kleinen Kunststoffgläser sind in unregelmäßigen Abständen auf der umgedrehten Zinkwanne mit Heißkleber befestigt. Je nach Tafellänge und Gästezahl haben mehrere der Arrangements auf einem Tisch Platz.

The tiny plastic glasses are hot-glued to the overturned zinc trough in a haphazard arrangement. Depending on the length of the table and the number of guests, several such arrangements will fit on the table.

Die Namensschilder schwingen an farbigem Draht und sind damit an Miniaturvasen befestigt. Diese sind mit gefärbtem Wasser sowie einer farblich passenden Blüte gefüllt.

The name tags swing gaily on coloured wires, attached to miniature vases. The glasses are filled with coloured water and sport flowers in matching shades.

Glanzlichter am Abend entstehen, wenn man zwischen den Blütengläschen auch Gläser mit Teelichtern platziert. Sie werden ebenfalls mit gefärbtem Wasser gefüllt und die Teelichter mit ihren Aluschälchen im oberen Drittel der Gläser eingeklemmt.

Evening highlights are created by placing glasses with tea lights between the ones with flowers inside. They are also filled with coloured water and the candle in its aluminium cup is placed in the upper third of the glass.

23

Blütenbündel
mit natürlichem Charme

floral bundles
with natural charm

Natürliche Gefäße. Wenn draußen unter freiem Himmel gefeiert wird, passt eine natürlich wirkende Dekoration am besten. Warum sollen da nicht auch die Gefäße direkt aus der Natur stammen? Die hohlen Halme von *Fallopia japonica* eignen sich perfekt als dekorative Vasenröhrchen. Das Laub der häufig an Straßenrändern wachsenden Staude wird dazu vollständig entfernt. Die Halme lassen sich mit einer Rosenschere in kürzere Abschnitte zerteilen. Je nach Höhe, geben sie dann sogar langstieligen Blüten den nötigen Halt. Ob einzeln oder gleich bündelweise verarbeitet, hängt vom gewünschten Gesamteindruck ab. Obwohl sehr einfach in der Handhabung, wird eine Gestaltung mit *Fallopia* ihre verblüffende Wirkung in keinem Fall verfehlen.

Natural containers. If you're going to have a party under the open sky, natural-looking decorations are best suited. So why shouldn't the containers themselves be borrowed straight from Mother Nature? The hollow stalks of *Fallopia japonica* make ideal decorative vases. The foliage of this hardy perennial, often found growing in ditches along country roads, must first be removed. For best results cut up the stalks into smaller pieces with secateurs. Depending on the length the stalk, it will give even long-stemmed flowers the support they need. The florals can be arranged singly or in bundles, depending on personal taste and the look you're going for. A stunning design idea with *Fallopia* that is astonishingly easy to make. Your guests will be charmed!

Fallopia im Bündel. Mehrere der Halmabschnitte gebündelt ersetzen eine mittelgroße Vase und bringen die Blütenkombination in Gelb–Weiß gut zur Geltung. Pro Tisch für sechs bis acht Personen sollten mindestens sechs der Blütenbündel gefertigt werden, die auf schlichte Topfuntersetzer aus glasiertem Ton gestellt werden. Das passt zum lässigen und rustikaleren Charakter einer Open-Air-Dekoration.

Fallopia in bunches. A handful of *Fallopia* stalks cut to size and bundled together will do the job of a medium-sized vase and beautifully enhance flower combinations in yellow-and-white.
For each table with six to eight place settings, at least six such arrangements will be needed. Display them on simple saucers of glazed clay – the perfect complement to the relaxed and rustic character of an open-air decoration.

Dickere und dünnere *Fallopia*-Halme werden mit Rebenbindegarn zu Bündeln zusammengefasst. Auf Akkuratesse kommt es hierbei nicht an, die Abschnitte können ruhig unterschiedlich lang sein, das unterstreicht die natürliche Wirkung. Die meisten Blüten sind direkt in die wassergefüllten Halme eingestellt. Einige langstielige sind zwischen die *Fallopia*-Abschnitte geklemmt und beziehen ihr Wasser aus der Tonschale.

Fallopia stalks of all thicknesses are bundled together and secured with florists' twine. Accuracy isn't so important here: the stalks can vary in length, as this will emphasise the natural look of the design. Most of the flowers are arranged right in the water-filled tubes, while a few long-stemmed elements are inserted between the *Fallopia* stalks and standing in water in the clay dish.

Die Halme lassen sich einfach verarbeiten. Die mit einer Rosenschere gekürzten Fallopia–Abschnitte zunächst mit einem oder mehreren Haushaltsgummibändern bündeln.

Fallopia stalks are very easy to work with. Once they have been shortened to the desired length, the stalks are first bundled together and secured with household rubber bands.

Anschließend die Bündel mehrfach mit Rebenbindegarn umwickeln, so dass die Gummibänder verdeckt werden. Die Bunde auf einen Tonuntersetzer stellen, mit Hilfe einer Pipettenflasche mit Wasser füllen und die Blüten einstellen.

Then the bundles are wrapped with several loops of florists' twine, making sure to conceal the rubber bands. Stand the bundles on clay saucers, fill with water with the help of a pipette and arrange the flowers inside.

Farbige Drahtgimpe hält die Serviette zusammen. Ein Stück *Fallopia*-Halm wird mit einem Messer bis zur Mitte eingeschnitten und über die Gimpe gezogen.

The serviette is rolled and secured with coloured wired gimp. A piece of *Fallopia* is split along one side to the centre and slipped over the band of gimp.

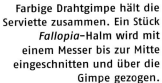

Fallopia im Topf. Verspielter und kleinteiliger wirkt diese Dekorationsvariante mit vielen kleinen Tontöpfen, die mit Abtönfarbe gestrichen sind. Quarzsand dient der Beschwerung und fixiert gleichzeitig die *Fallopia*-Halme, die mit Hilfe einer Pipettenflasche zunächst mit Wasser und anschließend mit Blüten gefüllt werden. Eine Dekorationsidee, die sich je nach Tischgröße beliebig erweitern lässt.

Potted Fallopia. This decoration alternative has a playful and delicate appearance with its many small clay pots, painted in matching shades. Quartz sand serves to weigh down the pots and at the same time anchors the *Fallopia* stalks, which are then filled with water with the help of a pipette and then adorned with flowers. A great decoration idea that can be expanded to fit any size table.

Bevor die *Fallopia*-Abschnitte im sandgefüllten Topf fixiert werden, müssen die Löcher im Topfboden mit Klebeband verschlossen werden. Zum Schluss wird die sandige Oberfläche mit fein geschnittener *Fallopia* abgestreut.

Before the *Fallopia* stalks can be secured in the sand-filled pot, the hole in the bottom of the pot must first be taped shut. As a final touch, the surface of the sand is strewn with tiny pieces of *Fallopia*.

Farbige Drahtgimpe hält die aufgerollten Stoffservietten zusammen. Die Drahtenden sind zu dekorativen Spiralen geformt, unter denen einzelne Hirse-Rispen durchgezogen werden.

Coloured wired gimp holds the rolled-up cloth serviettes together. The ends of stub wires are bent into decorative spirals, through which individual panicles of grain are threaded.

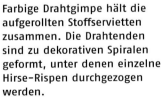

Auch für die Tischkarten werden die Topflöcher mit Klebeband verschlossen und die *Fallopia*-Stücke mit Sand fixiert. Die laminierten Namensschilder werden durch einen gespleißten Halm festgehalten.

Same procedure for the place cards: cover the hole in the bottom of the pot with tape and "plant" a *Fallopia* stalk in sand in the pot. The laminated name tag is wedged in a vertical slit in the top of the tube.

Fallopia als Kerzenschmuck. Für Feierlichkeiten, die bis in die Abendstunden andauern oder sogar erst am Abend beginnen, sollten immer Kerzen bei der Dekoration mit eingeplant werden. Auch dabei dient *Fallopia* als Basis für den rahmenden Blütenschmuck, der dicke Stumpenkerzen umgibt. Für eine Tafel mit sechs Personen sollten mindestens vier dieser Arrangements gefertigt werden.

Fallopia as a candle adornment. For celebrations that go on until dusk or do not begin until evening, candles should always be planned into the decorations. Here again, *Fallopia* forms the basis for the floral arrangement surrounding the thick pillar candles. For a table of six at least four such assemblies should be done up.

Die Kerzen erhalten einen
Ring aus *Fallopia*, der mit
Haushaltsgummiband und
Rebenbindegarn fixiert wird.
Die grün-weiße Blütenmischung
wird kurzstielig in die
Pflanzenröhrchen gestellt,
so dass nur die Blütenköpfe
herausschauen.

The candles are dressed up with
rings of *Fallopia* stalks, which
are bundled together and secured
first with rubber bands and then
florists' twine. The green-and white
mix of flowers have their stems
trimmed short and are inserted
inside the tubes with only the
flower heads visible.

Glänzende Drahtgimpe hält
die gerollten Stoffservietten
zusammen und ist am Ende
zu einer dekorativen Spirale
geformt. Einzelne Margeritenblüten werden als Schmuck
unter der Gimpe durchgezogen.

Shiny wired gimp holds the rolled-
up cloth serviette together and is
twirled into a decorative spiral at
one end. A single marguerite daisy
is pinned under the spiral and the
band of gimp.

Offizielle Anlässe

Firmenfeier – Mitarbeiterjubiläum – Empfang

Im allgemeinen fällt die Dekoration bei offiziellen Anlässen üppiger und repräsentativer aus, als bei Feiern im privaten Rahmen. Selbst in wirtschaftlich schlechteren Zeiten kommt es dabei oft nicht auf jeden Cent an und man ist – nicht zuletzt wegen der steuerlichen Absetzbarkeit – häufig bereit, etwas mehr in einen ansprechenden Blumenschmuck zu investieren. Denn Blumen gelten bei der Selbstdarstellung eines Unternehmens eindeutig als Sympathieträger. Ein Aspekt, den sich Floristen zunutze machen sollten. Wie die Dekoration für firmenbezogene Anlässe stilistisch ausfällt, hängt meist von der Branchenzugehörigkeit des jeweiligen Unternehmens und der Altersstruktur seiner Mitarbeiter ab. So wird ein traditionsreiches, angesehenes Bankhaus vermutlich anders feiern, als eine junge, angesagte Werbeagentur. Hier liegt gleichzeitig auch die Chance, mit der Art des Blumenschmucks unmittelbaren Bezug zum Unternehmen herzustellen, evtl. sogar dessen Produkte in die Dekoration mit einzubeziehen. Eine Herausforderung für jeden Floristen, bei der von dezent, förmlich, traditionell bis auffällig oder avantgardistisch gestalterisch alles möglich ist.

Generally speaking, the floral decorations for official occasions are more luxuriant and prestigious than for a party in a private setting. Even in an economic downturn most firms are not counting every cent and are often prepared to invest a bit more for the perfect floral arrangement – after all such an expense is a tax write-off. And when it comes to corporate identity flowers are clearly considered to be good for one's image. An aspect that florists should take advantage of. The exact design of decorations for company-related occasions usually depends on the type of firm, the sector it belongs to and the age structure of the staff. For example a respectable banking house, steeped in tradition, will presumably organise a different kind of function than the bash of a young, up-and-coming ad agency. Here also lies your chance to not only streamline the design of the floral decorations to the corporate image of your customer, but also to integrate some of their own products into your assemblies in an eye-catching way. This poses a real challenge for every florist, with the creative scope ranging from subdued, formal and traditional to over-the top or avant-garde.

official occasions

company function – anniversary – reception

Orchideen
in gediegener Eleganz

orchids
in tasteful elegance

Blüten mit Renommee. Orchideen eignen sich ausgezeichnet für einen eleganten, Exklusivität versprechenden Auftritt. Obwohl mittlerweile auch bei uns für jeden erschwinglich, gelten die Pflanzen mit ihren langen, dekorativen Blütenrispen als besonders wertvoll und edel. Gediegen wirkt die Dekoration, wenn Orchideen in Weiß, Aprikot- oder zarten Rosétönen für die Gestaltung gewählt werden. Alle weiteren Accessoires und verwendeten Materialien sollten die pudrigpastellige Ausstrahlung unterstützen. Der niveauvollen Gestaltung entsprechend, wirkt hochwertiges Porzellan in Weiß oder Creme am besten. Die Auswahl des Geschirrs kann im Vorfeld mit dem Restaurant oder Caterer abgesprochen und gegebenenfalls farblich auf die Blumendekoration abgestimmt werden. Das garantiert eine konsequente und überzeugende Gesamtwirkung.

Flowers with a reputation. Orchids are excellently suited for an elegant show with exclusive style. A once unaffordable luxury, these plants are no longer so expensive, yet with their long, decorative floral panicles they are still viewed as high-value and sophisticated. For an especially tasteful and up-market look, use orchids in shades of white, apricot or pale rosé for the table decorations. All other accessories and materials should further underscore the powdery-pastel ambience of the florals. The best match for such classy decorations are high-quality porcelain containers in white or crème. The choice of the tableware can be discussed beforehand with the restaurant or caterer and also be coordinated with the colours of the floral decorations. This will guarantee a consistent and convincing overall effect.

Topf-Orchideen in Festrobe. Wie elegant ein Tischschmuck aus Topfpflanzen ausfallen kann, verdeutlicht dieser Dekovorschlag mit Orchideen. Der Einsatz von Topfpflanzen hat gleichzeitig den Vorteil, dass sich die Dekoration früh-zeitig vorbereiten lässt, lange frisch bleibt und auch nach der Veranstaltung noch weiter verwendet werden kann. Auch die ausgefallenen, mit Blättern beklebten Übertöpfe können lange vor der Feier hergestellt werden.

Pot orchids in formal dress. Just how elegant a table decoration of potted plants can look is clearly demonstrated by this orchid idea. Using pot plants has the added advantage that the decoration can be made up in advance, will stay fresh longer and can also be put to further use after the event. Even the eye-catching pots with their covering of glued leaves can be prepared long before the day of the party.

Eine einzelne Orchideenblüte, in eine Spirale aus Golddraht eingeklemmt, dient als edle Tischkarte. Das gelochte Namensschild wird einfach auf den Draht gefädelt. Damit die Blüte nicht zu schnell austrocknet, sollte ihr Stielende kurz in flüssiges Wachs getaucht werden.

A single orchid flower, held aloft by a spiral of gold wire, serves as an elegant place card. Simply punch a hole in the name tag and thread a wire through it. To prevent the flower from drying out too quickly, its stem should be dipped briefly in liquid wax beforehand.

Die Löcher im Boden der Tontöpfe mit wasserfestem Tape verschließen. Die Stiele der Stachys-Blätter mit einer Schere abschneiden.

Seal the hole in the bottom of the clay pot with waterproof tape. Cut off the stems of the Stachys leaves with a pair of scissors.

Die Stachys-Blätter mit Sprühkleber schuppenartig auf die Töpfe kleben. Dabei am oberen Topfrand beginnen und die Blätter um die Kante herumschlagen.

Arrange the Stachys leaves in an overlapping pattern around the outside of the pot and affix with spray glue. Start at the rim of the pot and fold the uppermost row inwards over the edge.

Stachys-Blätter bilden nicht nur die dekorative Topfverkleidung, sondern auch einen zusätzlichen Kranzschmuck, der um die Töpfe gelegt wird. Als Kranzunterlage dient Draht, der mit *Tillandsia usneoides* umwickelt wird. Die Erde in den Töpfen ist ebenfalls mit *Tillandsia usneoides* und rosafarbenen Pfefferbeeren abgedeckt.

Stachys leaves not only comprise the fancy dress for the pots, but also the covering on additional wreath decorations that are arranged around the pots. The wreath base is a wire ring wrapped in *Tillandsia usneoides*. The soil in the pots is also strewn with *Tillandsia usneoides* and pink pepper berries.

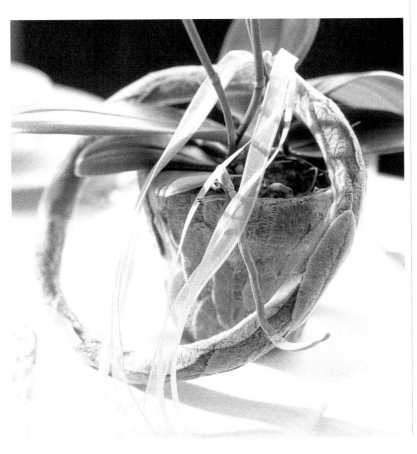

Orchideen als Schnittblume im Glas. Diese Dekoration lässt sich schnell vor Ort gestalten. Verschiedene Orchideen werden in schlichte, hohe Glasvasen eingestellt und mit exotischem Schnittgrün ergänzt. Teelichter in türkischen Teegläsern sind eine simple aber dennoch edle Beleuchtung für den Abend. Goldene Spindeln aus Draht, die zusätzlichen Glanz verleihen, können schon Tage vorher in Serie gefertigt werden.

Orchids as cut flowers in glass vases. This decoration can be done up in a wink right on the spot. Mixed orchids are arranged in tall, simple glass vases and complemented with exotic cut foliage. Tea lights in Turkish tea glasses make a simple yet elegant illumination for the evening. Gilded spindles of deco wire, which add extra pomp and shine, can be whipped up in sets a day or two before the party.

Die Spindel aus gebleichtem Weidenstab und Golddraht verrät den Gästen, an welchem Tisch sie sitzen. Sie wird zusammen mit den Orchideen in eine Vase gestellt.

A spindle of bleached wicker wrapped in gold reel wire, standing in one of the orchid vases, holds a list telling the guests where they are to sit.

Aus goldenem Schmuckdraht eine Spindel formen. Dabei den Schmuckdraht nach und nach von der Spule abwickeln und erst zum Schluss abschneiden.

Mould a spindle shape of gold deco wire, unspooling the wire from the reel as you go. When the desired spindle size has been achieved, cut the wire.

Für die feste Sitzordnung, können die einzelnen Namensschilder an einer Spindel aus Golddraht befestigt und unter den Serviettenring geschoben werden.

For indicating a more detailed seating arrangement, individual name tags can be attached to smaller spindles of gold reel wire and slipped inside the serviette rings.

Die Spindel auf einen gebleichten Weidenstab schieben und endgültig in Form bringen. Als Abschluss von oben (beim Serviettenschmuck auch von unten) eine Schmucknadel mit Perle auf den Stab ziehen. Das Namensschild fixieren, eventuell zusätzlich schmale Bänder an der Spindel befestigen.

Insert a bleached wicker stick in one end of the spindle and finish off the tapered tip. As a final touch add a decorative pin with a pearl to the top (on the serviette decorations to the bottom) end of the creation. Attach the name tag, if desired hang some thin ribbons from the tip of the spindle.

Ähren

rustikal und natürlich

wheat

rustic and natural

Ländliche Dekoration für die Erntezeit. Ähren eignen sich besonders für Tischdekorationen im Spätsommer und Herbst. Zwar sind sie in getrockneter Form das ganze Jahr über erhältlich. Dem Geschmack des Auftraggebers werden Floristen damit jedoch am besten in der entsprechenden Saison gerecht. Firmen, die der Bäckerszunft oder der Land–wirtschaft verbunden sind, stellen sicherlich Ausnahmen dar, für die sich mit einer solchen Dekoration auch ganzjährig der persönliche Bezug zum Unternehmen herstellen lässt. Für alle anderen vermitteln Ähren meist solide Bodenständigkeit und werden, speziell in Kombination mit anderen Herbstblühern, naturverbundene und traditionsbewusste Menschen in besonderem Maße begeistern.

Country decoration for harvest time. Ears of wheat are particularly well-suited for themed table decorations in late summer and autumn. Although they are available in dried form all year round, florists are well-advised to use them for symbolising the harvest season. Corporate customers in the baking industry or agriculture-related sectors may well be exceptions to this rule, where decorations based on such a theme may be popular all year round. For others, ears of wheat usually convey an impression of a solid establishment, and are very popular among nature-loving and tradition-conscious customers, especially in combination with other autumn bloomers.

Ähren als Rahmen für herbstliche Blüten. Zeitgemäß wirkt die Ährendekoration in schlichten Vasen, die in kleinen Gruppen auf dem Tisch platziert werden. Die Weizenähren werden mit Haushaltsgummis außen an den Gefäßen befestigt und mit breitem Karoband kaschiert. Im Gegensatz zur Blütenmischung in den Gläsern benötigen die Ähren keine Wasserversorgung.

Grain as a frame for autumn flowers. For a very contemporary look, place wheat decorations in simple vases and place in small groups on the table. Individual ears of wheat are arranged around the outside of the glass and affixed with household rubber bands, which are then concealed with red-and-white checked ribbon. Contrary to the flower arrangements inside the glasses, dried grain needs no water supply.

Die schlichten Vasen lassen sich mit einer Körnerfüllung schnell in außergewöhnliche Kerzenhalter verwandeln. Auf die losen Körner werden mit kariertem Band umwickelte Teelichter gesetzt.

Such simple vases can also be transformed into eye-catching candleholders in a wink. Fill the glass with loose kernels, set a tea light with a red-and-white checked ribbon around it on top.

Als Tischkarten dienen kleine Kränzchen aus Weizenähren mit rot–weiß kariertem Band. Die Namensschilder sind mit Hilfe von Schmucknadeln am Kranz befestigt.

For matching place cards, construct a small wreath of wheat ears and attach a red-and-white checked ribbon. The name tags are affixed to the wreaths with the help of decorative pins.

Ähren als herbstlicher Akzent im Fries. Deutlich traditioneller und rustikaler fällt dieser Tischschmuck in Form von niedrigen Gestecken aus. Als Unterlage für die Steckmasse dienen Terrakotta-Tabletts. Die gesteckte, herbstliche Blüten- und Beerenmischung wird zum Schluss mit Weizenähren „gespickt". Einzelne Ähren und Früchte sind lose über den Tisch gestreut.

Wheat as an autumn accent in a frieze. Clearly more traditional and rustic is this centrepiece in the form of a low table runner. The arrangement is based on floral foam on a terracotta tray. The based autumn flowers and berry combination is dotted with tiny ears of wheat. Individual ears of wheat and fruit and also strewn loosely over the table.

Neben Weizenähren bestimmen herbstliche Blüten wie Dahlien und Chrysanthemen, aber auch einige Freilandrosen, Disteln, *Heuchera*-Blätter und Beeren die ländlich-rustikale Wirkung des Tischschmucks.

In addition to the ears of wheat, autumn flowers such dahlias and chrysanthemums, field roses, thistles, *Heuchera* leaves and berries underscore the country look of the table decoration.

Kleine Erntekränze aus Weizen-ähren umgeben die Servietten. Ein Stück rot-weiß kariertes Band dient als farbiger Akzent und wird einfach um den Kranz geschlungen.

Miniature harvest wreaths of ears of wheat encircle the serviettes. A piece of red-and-white checked ribbon serves as a colour highlight and is simply looped around the wreath.

Rote Äpfel werden mit ange-drahteten Namenschildern zu originellen Tischkarten. Die Früchte müssen keine perfekte Form haben, sollten jedoch frei von faulen Stellen oder anderen Beschädigungen sein.

Red apples play the role of original place cards: The name tag dangles on a wire attached to the stem. The fruit needn't have a perfect shape, but should look appetizing, i.e. free of bruises or other blemishes.

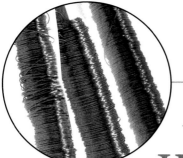

Drahtschmuck
für bunte Blüten

wire decorations
for bright blooms

Drahtgeflecht als Schmuckstück für den Tisch. Jüngere Unternehmen erweisen sich im Allgemeinen etwas aufgeschlossener gegenüber ausgefalleneren Dekorationen. Da können auch mal außergewöhnliche Materialien und Formen, sowie gewagte Blüten- und Farbkombinationen ins Spiel gebracht werden. Schmuckdraht, den es mittlerweile in vielen knalligen Farben gibt, bietet sich für eine Dekoration in ungewohnter Optik an und wird garantiert für Aufsehen sorgen. Früher lediglich als Hilfsmittel zur Befestigung floraler Werkstoffe verwendet, darf er heute als gestalterisches Element ebenso stark wirken, wie die Blüten selbst. Seine Verarbeitungsmöglichkeiten sind in der modernen Floristik äußerst vielfältig. Für eines ist er jedoch in jedem Fall zu schade: zum Verstecken.

Intertwined wire gems for the table. Younger business people generally prove somewhat more open-minded as regards off-the-wall decorations. For such customers more unusual materials and shapes, as well as daring flowers and colour combinations, can come into play. Decorative wire and finer metallic thread, these days available in lots of bright colours, are just the ticket for table decorations with unusual flair, guaranteed to turn heads. Formerly used only as mechanics for securing florals, reel wire is being used more and more as a creative element that is just an essential part of the assembly as the flowers themselves. The range of possibilities for working with wire in modern floristry is almost endless. One thing you shouldn't do with it is hide it!

Gefäßummantelung mit Schmuckdraht. Aus schlichten, kubischen Glasgefäßen werden wahre Eyecatcher, wenn sie mit farbigem Schmuckdraht ummantelt und mit Frühlings- blüten gefüllt werden. Als Reihung in der Tafelmitte kommen sie am besten zur Geltung. Zwischen den selbst gestalteten, ummantelten Vasen finden sich auch passende Drahtgefäße als Kerzenhalter, die als Fertigprodukt im Handel erhältlich sind und damit zusätzliche Arbeit ersparen.

Vase encirclements with deco wire. You can transform simple, boxy glass containers into real eye-catchers by dressing them up with webs of colourful reel wire and filling them with spring blooms. Lined up in a row along the centre of the table they will make a beautiful centrepiece. Between the vases with their hand- made wire encirclements you can add some ready-made matching wire containers; integrating a few retail products saves you time and additional work.

Der Draht dient nicht nur als dekorative Ummantelung der unterschiedlich hohen Glasgefäße, sondern wird als locker verwobenes Knäuel in der Vase auch als Steckhilfe für die Blüten genutzt. Die Auswahl der Blütenfarben beschränkt sich bewusst auf Pink-, Rot-, Orange- und Gelbtöne, die sich in der Farbe des Schmuckdrahtes wiederholen.

The wire not only serves as a decorative covering on glass containers of varying sizes, but also as a loosely-woven grid inside the vase to give the flowers extra support. The choice of flower colours is purposely restricted to the pink, red, orange and yellow spectrum to reflect the colour of the decorative wire.

Auch der Serviettenschmuck ist aus Draht gefertigt. Eine einzelne *Clivia*-Blüte wird darin eingeklemmt. Ihr Stiel ist mit Schlagmetall vergoldet.

The serviette decorations are flat, moulded squares of reel wire. A single *Clivia* flower, its stem gilded with a shiny layer of gold leaf, is pinned to the cushion with a single wire.

Kleine Würfel aus farbigem Schmuckdraht halten die gelochten Namensschilder und sind schnell mit der Hand geformt. Die Farbe der Würfel kann, wie auch bei den Gefäßummantelungen, variieren.

Small cubes of coloured deco wire hold the name tags via punched holes and can be moulded into shape by hand in no time. As with the vase decorations, the colour of the cubes can vary.

Drahtkugeln als Blütenhalter. Unbeschwerte Fröhlichkeit strahlen die trendigen Kugeln mit Mohnblütenfüllung aus. Werden sie, wie hier, auf einem Läufer in der Tischmitte arrangiert, sollte man, für einen optimalen Gesamteindruck, mindestens zwei Kugeln pro Person fertigen.

Wire balls as flower holders. These trendy spheres with their single poppies radiate a carefree party atmosphere. When arranged down the centre of a long table for optimal impact, as we have done here, at least two assemblies per person should be calculated.

Die Drahtkugeln werden mit der Hand geformt und die Reagenzgläser für die Wasserversorgung der Mohnblüten in der Mitte eingeklemmt. Einzelne Halme Steelgras sind zwischen das Drahtgeflecht der Kugeln als farblicher Akzent eingewoben.

The wire balls are moulded by hand and the glass tubes for water for the poppies are integrated in the top. Individual blades of *Xanthorrhoea australis* interwoven through the wire mesh to add colour highlights.

Die kleineren Kugeln für die Tischkarten werden in der gleichen Technik wie die großen hergestellt. Statt Reagenzgläsern sichern Orchideenröhrchen die Wasserversorgung der Tulpenblüten.

The smaller balls for the place cards are constructed using the same technique as the larger ones. Instead of glass tubes, here smaller orchid tubes provide the water supply for the tulips.

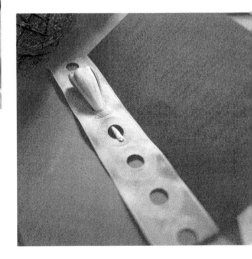

Die Menükarte ziert ein breites, gelochtes Schmuckband, in das eine einzelne Blüte eingeklemmt wird. Das Band eignet sich auch als Serviettenring.

The menu is adorned with a wide strip of ribbon dotted with a row of punched holes, with a single flower threaded through the holes. This ribbon also makes a suitable serviette ring.

Füllhörner aus Schmuckdraht. Der farbige Draht ist ein echter Verwandlungskünstler. In gleicher Technik wie die Kugeln auf der Vorseite werden hier kleine Füllhörner zum unkonventionellen und verspielten Tischschmuck. Sie variieren in Größe und Farbe und werden durch niedrige, farbige Gläser mit Teelichtern ergänzt. Eine Dekoration, deren Gesamtwirkung sehr unkompliziert ist, die allerdings in der Herstellung der Füllhörner ein wenig Fingerfertigkeit erfordert.

Wire horns of plenty. Coloured reel wire is a real quick-change artist. Constructed using the same technique as for the balls on the previous page, here small harvest horns make unconventional and playful table decorations. They vary in size and colour and are complemented by small coloured glasses with tea lights. A table decoration with a very uncomplicated look, although a bit of dexterity is necessary to achieve the desired shape.

Ranunkeln in Orange- und Rottönen bilden die frühlingshafte Füllung der Drahthörnchen. Der Rand der Füllhörner ist mit Steelgras durchwoben und so besonders betont.

Buttercups in shades of orange and red form the springtime filling of the wire horns. The rim of the horn is interwoven with a blade of *Xanthorrhoea australis* for an extra, natural highlight.

Für die Füllhörner werden Schmuckdraht, je ein Orchideenröhrchen, eine Ranunkelblüte und Steelgras benötigt.

For each horn of plenty you will need coloured reel wire, an orchid tube, a buttercup flower and Xanthorrhoea australis.

Aus dem Schmuckdraht ein Füllhorn formen. Den Rand mit Steelgras durchweben und die Ranunkelblüte im Orchideenröhrchen einsetzen.

Mould a horn of plenty of deco wire. Interweave the rim with Xanthorrhoea australis and arrange a buttercup in an orchid tube inside the horn.

Die kleinen Füllhörner für die Tischkarten werden in der gleichen Technik wie die großen gefertigt. Die Namensschilder aus farbigem Papier sind mit einer Schmucknadel daran befestigt.

The small wire horns for the place cards are constructed using the same technique as the larger ones. The name tags of coloured paper are pinned to the horns with decorative pins.

Blütenwürfel

in grafischer Strenge

floral cubes

in strict graphic form

Klare Formen für moderne Blütenkompositionen. Klare Umrisslinien und geometrische Formen wirken bei der Gestaltung mit natürlichen Werkstoffen meist sehr gestylt und konstruiert. Bei Tischdekorationen in einem modernen Ambiente kann aber gerade dieser Effekt besonders reizvoll und erwünscht sein. Viereck- oder Würfelformen stehen in interessantem Kontrast zur natürlichen, rundlichen Form vieler Blüten. Auch die Beschränkung auf nur zwei Farben, wie zum Beispiel Grün und Weiß, verstärkt den modernen, puristischen Gesamteindruck einer Dekoration und lässt sie äußerst elegant und edel erscheinen.

Clear shapes for modern floral assemblies. Clear outlines and geometric shapes, in combination with natural materials, usually create a high-styled and constructed look. An effect that can be especially charming and popular for table decorations in a modern atmosphere. Squares or cube shapes stand in interesting contrast to the natural, round shapes of many flowers. Add to that the restriction to two colours, for example green and white, and the modern, purist ambience of such decorations can achieve an extremely elegant and noble look.

Gefüllte Blattwürfel. Die Tischdekoration aus Steckschaum-würfeln, die mit *Aspidistra*- und Efeu-Blättern verkleidet werden, wirkt besonders modern. In ihrer strengen Anord-nung und in der Reduzierung auf wenige Farbtöne erscheint sie fast asiatisch. Selbst die Kerzenhalter reihen sich in Gestaltung und Form in das strenge Schema ein. Vier der Blattwürfel bilden jeweils eine Einheit und werden pass-genau in eine quadratische Aluminiumwanne gesetzt.

Filled leafy cubes. This table decoration of floral foam cubes, covered with *Aspidistra* and ivy leaves, has a particularly modern look. Thanks to its strict arrangement and the reduction to very few colours, it has almost Asiatic flair. Even the candleholders are in line with the strict scheme of the design. Each group of four floral cubes forms a unit and fits perfectly in the square aluminium trays.

Bei den Tischkarten wiederholt sich die Form von Würfel und Quadrat. Je ein Stück Pergaminpapier und *Aspidistra*-Blatt werden aufeinander gelegt und mit einer Niete versehen. Durch die Öse wird ein Band geknotet, das Papier beschriftet und in einen handelsüblichen Fotohalter geklemmt.

The place cards again repeat the square and cubist design of the decoration. Each one is made by laying a piece of parchment on a square of *Aspidistra* leaf, and pinning them together with a metal rivet. A ribbon is knotted through the hole in the rivet, the name is printed on the paper and the name tag is clipped in a store bought photo holder.

Für die Blattwürfel werden Efeu- oder Aspidistra-Blätter, Stecknadeln, Steckschaumwürfel und getrocknete weiße Bohnen benötigt.

For the leafy cube you will need ivy or Aspidistra leaves, straight pins and floral foam cubes as well as dried white beans.

Den Steckschaum mit den Blättern und Stecknadeln ummanteln. Den Rand oben etwas überstehen lassen und mit der Schere begradigen. Eine Anemonenblüte oder eine mit Steckdraht versehene Stumpenkerze im Steckschaum fixieren und die noch sichtbare Oberfläche mit Bohnen abstreuen.

Cover the floral foam cube with the leaves and secure with pins. Allow the top edge to stand up a bit higher and then trim evenly with scissors. Anchor an anemone flower or a pillar candle on a stub wire in the foam and conceal the surface of the foam with beans.

Der puristische Serviettenschmuck besteht aus ausgeschnittenem Fotokarton und einem Stück *Aspidistra*-Blatt. Mit Sprühkleber miteinander verbunden, wird die Dekoration mit einem schmalen Band versehen und dieses mit einer Schmucknadel an der Serviettenhaube befestigt.

The purist serviette decoration consists of a cut square of card and a piece of *Aspidistra* leaf. Stuck together with spray glue, the decoration is adorned with a narrow ribbon and then pinned to the folded serviette with a straight pin.

Holzwürfel mit Silber veredelt. Die elegante Wirkung dieses Tischschmucks entsteht durch seine aufstrebende und grafische Gestaltung, sowie durch die verwendeten, besonders edlen Werkstoffe und Materialien. Irisblüten und französische Tulpen werden in Reagenzgläser eingestellt, die wiederum in versilberten Holzwürfeln verankert sind. In der Mitte des Tisches wiederholen würfelförmige, weiße Kerzen die Form im Kleinen.

Wooden cubes dressed in silver leaf. The elegant impact of this table decoration is created by its upright and graphic design, as well as the particularly elegant-looking florals and other materials used. Iris flowers and French tulips are arranged in parallel glass tubes anchored in wooden cubes covered in silver leaf. In the centre of the table, small white candles reflect the cubist design en miniature.

Holzwürfel sind mit silbernem Schlagmetall und Sprühkleber verkleidet. Die Vertiefungen für die Reagenzgläser werden mit dem Akkubohrer gebohrt. Da die Dekoration sehr hoch gestaltet ist, eignet sie sich am besten für die Seiten eines Tisches.

Spray the wooden cubes with adhesive and pat on a layer of silver leaf. Hollow out the centre for the test tubes with a cordless drill. As the decoration stands very tall, it is best placed along the edge of the table.

An die Serviettenhauben wird mit Büroklemmen je ein Bündel Steelgras geklemmt. Dies unterstützt die reduzierte und grafische Gesamtwirkung der Dekoration.

The folded serviette is adorned with a bundle of *Xanthorrhoea australis*, held in place by a bulldog clip. This reinforces the reduced and graphic look of the decoration.

Die Menüfolge entnehmen die Gäste einem beschrifteten Pergaminpapier, das mit einer großen Büroklemme an ein dünnes Holzbrett geheftet wird.

The menu can be read by the guests from a small sheet of parchment paper on a miniature "clipboard", made of a thin sheet of wood and a bulldog clip.

Blumenwiese
auf den Tisch gebracht

flower meadow
served at table

Blütenträume auf der grünen Wiese. Frisches, grünes Gras symbolisiert den Sommer. Seine Optik und sein Geruch erwecken Erinnerungen an ein Picknick bei strahlendem Sonnenschein, an entspanntes Im-Gras-Liegen oder den ersten selbstgepflückten Strauß des Geliebten. Wer also Sommergefühl pur in den Raum bringen möchte, liegt mit dieser Dekoration garantiert richtig. In ihrer Gestaltung gemäßigt und keinesfalls zu gewagt, eignet sie sich auch für offizielle Anlässe und sorgt allein durch ihren Anblick schon für positive Stimmung. Wiesengras und eine blau-weiße Blütenmischung sind die Basis für alle drei gezeigten Varianten, deren Form und Wirkung dennoch völlig unterschiedlich sind.

Floral dreams on a green meadow. Fresh green grass symbolises summertime. Its appearance and fragrance arouse memories of picnics under clear blue skies, of relaxing naps in verdant fields or the first hand-plucked bouquet from an admirer. Anyone wishing to bring these feelings indoors is sure to be intrigued by this decoration. Reserved in its design and by no means too daring, this decoration is also well-suited for official functions. Just one look at it will lift the spirits of all the guests. Meadow grass and a blue-and-white mix of flowers form the basis for all three of the variants shown here, although each has its own special form and impact.

Sträuße wie von der Wiese gepflückt. Die runden Blütenarrangements sehen aus, als stammten sie direkt von einer üppig blühenden Wiese. Doch wer genauer hinsieht, wird bemerken, dass bei weitem nicht alle verwendeten Blüten wirklich auf sommerlichen Wiesen zu finden sind. Die eine oder andere edlere Blüte fügt sich perfekt ein und wertet die Komposition zusätzlich auf.

Bouquets picked from the meadow. These circular floral arrangements look like they came straight from a luxuriant meadow in full bloom. But if you take a closer look you will notice that not all the flowers in the bouquets can really be found in summer fields. One or two more up-market blooms have been added to complement the bouquets perfectly and add value to the composition.

Schlichte Stumpenkerzen werden mit schlaufenförmig angelegtem Gras veredelt. Bei der Fixierung an der Kerze kommt ein Tacker zum Einsatz, eine Bandumwicklung verdeckt die Tackernadeln.

Simple pillar candles are given an elegant, ballooning frill of grass. The grass is simply stapled to the candle, with a loop of ribbon concealing the mechanics.

Das Gras um schlichte Glasvasen oder Trinkgläser legen und mit Haushaltsgummiband befestigen. Das Gummiband anschließend mit Schmuckband oder Bast kaschieren.

Arrange bunches of grass around simple glass vases or tumblers and secure with a household rubber band. Then conceal the rubber band with a loop of ribbon or raffia bast.

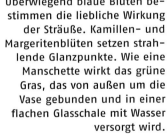

Das Gefäß mit Wasser füllen und so viele Blüten einzeln einstellen, dass eine üppige und ausgewogene Mischung entsteht.

Fill the container with water and insert the flowers individually until a generous and well-balanced bouquet is achieved.

Überwiegend blaue Blüten bestimmen die liebliche Wirkung der Sträuße. Kamillen- und Margeritenblüten setzen strahlende Glanzpunkte. Wie eine Manschette wirkt das grüne Gras, das von außen um die Vase gebunden und in einer flachen Glasschale mit Wasser versorgt wird.

Predominantly blue flowers determine the sweet impact of the bouquets. Camomile and Marguerite daisies provide brilliant highlights. Like a foliage collar the bunches of green grass surround the vegetative assembly, attached around the sides of the vase and standing in water in a shallow glass dish.

Ein Stück Blumenwiese als Fries. Diese Wiesenvariante eignet sich besonders für längere Tafeln und findet auch auf schmalen Tischen Platz. Je nach Personenzahl können auch mehrere der Blütenfriese aneinander gereiht werden. Das Wiesengras ist in Bündeln seitlich an einer länglichen Steckschaumschale mit Hilfe von Haften befestigt. Die blau–weiße Blütenmischung wird von oben in den Steckschaum gesteckt.

A bit of flower meadow as a frieze. This vegetative meadow alternative is particularly well-suited for longer tables, and even the narrowest table will be able to accommodate it. Depending on the number of guests, more than one floral frieze can be arranged end-to-end. The grass is tied in bundles and pinned along the sides of a longish floral foam dish. The blue-and-white floral mixture is inserted in the foam from the top.

Kleinen quadratischen Tellern auf jedem Tisch können die Gäste die Sitzordnung entnehmen. Rosafarbener Bast hält ein Grasbüschel, sowie das mit den Namen der Gäste beschriftete Tonpapier.

Guest lists on small square plates on every table tell the guests where they are to sit. A band of pink ribbon holds a tuft of grass in place beside a sheet of coloured paper on which the names of the guests are written.

Wichtig: Die Blütenmischung wirkt zwar insgesamt blau, dennoch sollten unbedingt auch einige weiße Blüten eingearbeitet werden. Das setzt Glanzpunkte und bringt den Blumenschmuck zum Strahlen.

Important: although the flower mix is in the blue range, integrating a few white flowers is an absolute must. This sets highlights of colour contrast in the focal area and adds rhythm.

Eine einzelne Margeritenblüte dient als lieblicher Serviettenschmuck. Der Blumenstiel wird mit Wiesengras und Band umwickelt. Eine aufgeklebte Perle veredelt die Dekoidee.

A single Marguerite daisy serves as a sweet serviette adornment. The stem of the flower is wound about with grass and a narrow ribbon. The tiny creation is finished off with a pearl glued on the ribbon.

Blumenwiese als Kerzenschmuck. Schlichte Stumpenkerzen werden mit blau-weißen Blütenkränzen auf Wiesengrasbasis geschmückt. Die Wiesenoptik tritt dabei zugunsten üppiger Blumenfülle deutlich zurück. Eine Dekorationsvariante, die sich sowohl für kleinere Tische, als auch für große Tafeln eignet, da sie sich beliebig fortführen lässt.

Flower meadow as a candle decoration. Simple pillar candles are adorned with blue-and-white floral wreaths on a base of meadow grass. This time the meadow theme is reduced in favour of a more opulent mix of flowers. A decoration variant that is well-suited for tables of any size, as it can be expanded indefinitely.

Den Blütenkränzen dient ein Steckschaumring als Basis. Dabei wird zuerst das Gras mit Haften seitlich am Steckschaum befestigt, anschließend die Blütenmischung von oben eingesteckt.

The floral wreath is based on a ring of floral foam. First the grass is pinned along the sides of the foam and then the flowers are inserted from the top.

Margeriten als Platzanweiser. Ein Orchideenröhrchen ist mit Gras und Band umwickelt und versorgt die Blüte mit Wasser. Mit Hilfe einer Schmucknadel werden Namensschild und Röhrchen vorsichtig am Stuhl befestigt.

Marguerite daisies as place cards. An orchid tube is encircled with grass and ribbon and serves as a water supply for the flower. With the help of a decorative pin the name tag and water tube are carefully attached to the back of the chair.

Natürliche Serviettenringe aus einem Bündel Wiesengras werden auf der Unterseite mit Myrtendraht zusammengefasst und über gerollte Stoffservietten geschoben.

Natural serviette rings of bunches of meadow grass are secured underneath with myrtle wire and slipped over the rolled-up cloth serviettes.

Weiße Feste

Hochzeit – Taufe – Kommunion – Konfirmation

Der Begriff „Weiße Feste" bezieht sich auf Feierlich-keiten, die ursprünglich mit einer kirchlichen Zeremonie in Verbindung standen, z. B. Taufen, Kommunion oder Konfirmation und vor allem natür-lich Hochzeiten. Zwar lassen sich immer weniger Paare heutzutage kirchlich trauen. Doch ob mit oder ohne den Segen der Kirche – auf die anschließende Feier hat dies meistens keinen großen Einfluss. Denn schließlich möchten auch diejenigen, die nur stan-desamtlich heiraten, dem Anlass einen entsprechen-den Rahmen verleihen und zusammen mit Freunden und Verwandten einen unvergesslichen Tag verbringen. Dazu gehört, neben Brautstrauß und Wagenschmuck, für die meisten auch eine festliche Tischdekoration. Eine besondere Herausforderung für den Floristen, denn bei kaum einem anderen Anlass sind die Kun-den bereit, so viel in Blumenschmuck zu investieren. Denn schließlich soll die eigene Hochzeit ja etwas ganz Besonderes sein. Die konkreten Vorstellungen eines Brautpaares lassen sich am besten in einem beratenden Gespräch vor Ort klären.

The term "white ceremony" refers to festivities that originally had to do with religious ceremonies, e.g. christenings, first Holy Communion or confirmation, and of course weddings. Although fewer couples are getting married in the church these days, the wedding reception is still a very important highlight, regardless of whether the blessing of the church plays a role. Because after all, even couples who say their vows at the registry office want to mark the occasion with a modicum of grandeur and spend an unforgettable day with friends and family. In addition to the bridal bouquet and floral decorations for the car, for most newlyweds the right table decorations are a must. A special challenge for every florist, as weddings are an occasion where customers are prepared to invest a bit more in their floral arrange-ments. Because after all, there is no day more special than one's own wedding day. The ideas and wishes of the bride- and groom-to-be are best discussed in a consulting session with the florist, if possible in the rooms where the reception is to be held.

white ceremonies

wedding – baptism – communion – confirmation

Blütenkränze

in Pastelltönen

floral wreaths

in pastel shades

Blütenkränze mit Symbolik. Kränze sind gerade für Hochzeiten eine häufig gewählte Dekorationsform. In ihrer Gestalt
– ohne Anfang und ohne Ende – greifen sie die Symbolik der
Eheringe auf und stehen für treue und immerwährende
Liebe. Bei der Gestaltung von Brautsträußen und Autoschmuck
wird diese Form daher immer wieder gerne aufgenommen.
Aber auch als symbolträchtige Tischdekoration sind Blütenkränze ein passender Schmuck für Hochzeiten. Gerade für
runde Tische bietet sich, statt eines gewöhnlichen Gesteckes
in der Tischmitte, ein großer gewundener oder gesteckter
Kranz an. Die Blütenauswahl kann individuell vorgenommen
werden, oftmals soll die Tischdekoration mit dem Strauß
der Braut harmonieren. Sehr edel und festlich wirken die
Tischkränze, wenn sie in hellen Pastelltönen gestaltet sind.

Floral wreaths with symbolism. Wreaths are the most popular
type of table decoration for weddings. The very shape of the
wreath – a circle without beginning or end – reflects the symbolism
of the wedding bands and stands for loyal and undying love.
Therefore it is an all-time favourite, not only for bridal bouquets
and wedding coach decorations, but also as a symbolic table decoration. Floral wreaths are almost a must for weddings. Round tables
are especially suitable for presenting large intertwined or foam-
based wreaths, as opposed to other centrepiece designs. The choice
of flowers can be made individually, and very often couples want
the table decoration to harmonise with the flowers in the bridal
bouquet. For a particularly elegant and festive look, such table
wreaths should be done up in pale pastel shades.

Gesteckter Blütenkranz. Ein Kranz, bei dem die Blüten dicht an dicht gesteckt werden, wirkt besonders üppig. Als Basis dient eine gut gewässerte Kranzunterlage aus Steckschaum, in die die Blütenmischung mit stark gekürzten Stielen gesteckt wird. Wichtig für die luftige Gesamtwirkung: Es sollten immer wieder grüne Blätter z. B. von *Alchemilla*, *Galax* oder Efeu zwischen die Blüten gesteckt werden.

Based floral wreath. A wreath of tightly massed flowers makes a very luxurious impression. This assembly is based on a well-soaked ring of floral foam, on which the mix of florals is arranged with the trimmed stems pushed firmly in the foam. Important for achieving a loose and airy look: as much as possible integrate green leaves, for example *Alchemilla*, *Galax* or ivy, between the flowers.

Ein handelsüblicher Kartenhalter in Herzform wird durch eine Vergoldung mit Schlagmetall zusätzlich veredelt. Feines Büttenpapier wird mit dem Namen des Gastes beschriftet und einfach eingeklemmt.

A standard commercial card holder in the shape of a heart is dressed up for the occasion with a layer of gold leaf. The names of the guests are written on a square of fine, handmade paper and simply clipped between the two sides of the holder.

Aus Schmuckdraht und einigen grünen Zweigen (z. B. von Rosmarin, Thymian oder Myrte) ein kleines Kränzchen wickeln. Ob goldener oder silberner Draht verwendet wird, hängt von der Farbigkeit des Deko-Pins ab.

Construct a tiny wreath of reel wire and a few green sprigs of foliage (e.g. rosemary, thyme or myrtle). Use either gold or silver wire, whichever matches the decorative pin.

Den Kranz auf den Pin schieben. Eventuell als unteren Abschluss eine Perle auffädeln und mit Heißkleber fixieren.

Skewer the wreath on the pin. For added stability, thread a bead on the lower end and affix with hot glue.

Auch der Serviettenschmuck greift in dekorativer Weise die Kranzform auf. Wer möchte, kann an dem perlenbesetzten Deko-Pin, der durch den kleinen Kranz gestochen wird, auch ein Namensschild befestigen.

Even the serviette adornment reflects the wreath form in a decorative way. If desired, the name tag can also be attached to the miniature wreath with the beaded pin.

Blattkranz mit Blütenfüllung. Auffällig und außergewöhnlich wirkt dieser Kranz, der nur in der Mitte mit Blüten gefüllt ist. Der Kranzkörper selbst wird mit ledrigen *Galax*-Blättern besteckt. Eine Dekorationsvariante, die sich wegen ihrer etwas wuchtigeren und kompakten Form gut für größere runde Tische eignet.

Foliage wreath with floral filling. For a really striking and unusual wreath, fill the centre of a foliage ring with flowers. The wreath itself is covered with a layer of leathery *Galax* leaves. A decoration alternative that is excellently suited for very large round tables, due to its massive and compact form.

Eine Kranzunterlage aus Steckschaum mit Galax-Blättern
und Schmucknadeln bestecken.
Dabei die Blätter überlappend
anordnen.

*Completely cover a floral foam wreath
form with Galax leaves and secure
with beaded pins. Arrange the leaves
in a flat, overlapping pattern.*

In der Mitte des Kranzes einen
Kunststoffteller mit gewässertem
Steckschaum positionieren.
Die Blüten kuppelförmig in den
Steckschaum stecken.

*In the centre of the wreath fit a
plastic dish with a well-soaked piece
of floral foam. Arrange the flowers in
a dome shape on the wet foam.*

**Als Tischkarten und gleichzeitige
Andenken für die Gäste
dienen kleine Schachteln mit
Mandeldragee-Füllung. Ein
Brauch, der in Italien und
Frankreich seit langem gepflegt
wird, und auch bei uns immer
beliebter wird.**

Small boxes of sugared almonds
serve as place cards and at the
same time wedding favours for the
guests. A custom long practised
in Italy and France that is also
becoming increasingly popular
in Germany.

Gewundener Blütenkranz. Obwohl der Kranz aus der gleichen Blütenmischung wie die beiden vorherigen besteht, ist seine optische Wirkung wesentlich leichter. Ausschlaggebend dafür sind unterschiedliche Fertigungstechniken. Dieser Kranz ist nicht gesteckt, sondern gewunden. Als Basis dient ein Gerüst aus *Clematis*- und Efeuranken.

Interwoven floral wreath. Although this wreath is made using the same floral mix as in the two previous assemblies, its optical effect is considerably lighter and more airy. This is due to the construction technique: This wreath is not based on floral foam but rather wound freehand. A ring of *Clematis* and ivy vines serves as the basis.

Wie im Großen, so im Kleinen. Auch die Platzkarten sind an kleinen Kränzen aus *Clematis*- und Efeuranken mit Band befestigt und mit einer Schmucknadel vorsichtig am Stuhl festgesteckt.

Same thing again en miniature. The place cards are also tiny wreaths of *Clematis* and ivy vines, with long flowing ribbons. They are carefully attached to the backs of the chairs with beaded pins.

Am Kranzgerüst aus *Clematis*- und Efeuranken sind Reagenzgläser mit Rebenbindegarn befestigt. Diese werden durch eine Pipettenflasche mit Wasser gefüllt und mit unterschiedlichen Blüten bestückt.

Attach a small glass tube with florists' twine to the wreath of *Clematis* and ivy vines. The tube is filled with water with a pipette and then an assortment of flowers is arranged inside.

Die Serviettenringe sind aus Rebenbindegarn geformt. Ein mit Schlagmetall vergoldetes Efeublatt wird mit seinem Stiel unter den Windungen durchgezogen.

The serviette rings are made of paper-covered wire. A layer of gold leaf is brushed on an ivy leaf and its stem is inserted between the wires.

Graslook
modern und avantgardistisch

grass look
modern and avant-garde

Blüten im grünen Grasmantel. Wer es bei der Tischdekoration geradliniger und weniger verspielt mag, wird sich vielleicht für diese Schmuckvariante begeistern können. Grünes Steel-gras und einzelne weiße Blüten sind hier für die reduzierte aber nicht minder festliche Wirkung der Dekoration maßgebend. Zwar finden weiße Blüten wegen ihres Symbolgehalts (Reinheit und Unschuld der Braut) von jeher in der Hochzeitsfloristik Verwendung, doch hat diese Dekoration mit der althergebrachten und traditionellen Sichtweise wenig gemein. In ihrer Reduziertheit und grafischen Strenge lässt sie vielmehr asiatische Gestaltungsprinzipien anklingen. Unbedingte Voraussetzung für solch einen Tafelschmuck ist allerdings ein entsprechend modernes Ambiente.

Flowers in green grass cloaks. For those who like table decorations with straight and simple lines, this version is sure to turn heads. Green steel grass and single white flowers characterise this minimalist but no less festive-looking decoration right down the line. Although white lilies have always found a niche in floral wedding design on account of their symbolism (purity and innocence of the bride), this decoration has little in common with old customs and traditional attitudes. In its restriction to only two florals and its graphic strictness, the style is more reminiscent of Asiatic principles of floral design. This type of idea should, however, be reserved for more modern interiors.

Hoch hinaus mit Gras und Blüten. Lange Gräser sowie Kalla- und Anthurienblüten lassen die Dekoration streng aber gleichzeitig auch elegant erscheinen. Die Grasbündel werden entlang der Tischmitte in einer Reihe angeordnet. Dabei sollte darauf geachtet werden, dass sich die jeweils gegenüber sitzenden Gäste noch sehen und ungestört unterhalten können.

Reaching up with grass and flowers. Long grasses with Calla lilies and *Anthurium* lend the table decoration a strict yet at the same time elegant ambience. The grass bundles are arranged in a row down the centre of the table. When positioning them, care should be taken to ensure that the guests will be able to see and converse with one another across the table, without being disturbed by the flowers.

Auch die Tischkarten bestehen aus kleinen Grasbündeln. Im Inneren sorgt ein mit Walzblei umlegtes Orchideenröhrchen für die Standfestigkeit. Außen dient ein Streifen Walzblei gleichermaßen zur Beschwerung und Fixierung der bündig geschnittenen Grasummantelung. Das Namensschild ist mit einer Perle auf einen längeren Grashalm gezogen und im Orchideenröhrchen verankert.

The place cards are also made of tiny bundles of chopped grass. Plastic orchid tubes are hidden inside and a band of rolled metal adds extra stability. Around the outside of the grass, additional bands of rolled metal serve to weight down the creations and also hold the grass bundles together. The name tag is threaded with a faux pearl on a longer blade of grass, which is anchored in the orchid tube.

Für die ummantelten Gefäße werden Steelgras, hohe zylindrische Glasvasen, Haushaltsgummibänder, Perlen und Walzblei (aus dem Baustoffhandel) benötigt.

For the grass-covered containers you will need Xanthorrhoea australis, tall cylindrical glass vases, rubber bands, beads and strips of rolled metal (builders' supply).

Mit Hilfe von Haushaltsgummibändern die Gräser um die Vasen legen. Die Gummibänder mit schmalen Walzbleistreifen verdecken. Auf einzelne Gräser Perlen fädeln. Die Gefäße mit Wasser füllen und je eine Kalla oder Anthurie einstellen.

First arrange the bundles of grass around the glass vases and secure with household rubber bands. Then conceal the rubber bands with strips of rolled metal. Thread faux pearls on individual blades of grass. Fill the vases with water and add either a single Calla lily or Anthurium.

Die Servietten erhalten ebenfalls einen Grasmantel. Dafür wird Katzengras laminiert und die Folie anschließend auf ein Format in Höhe der Servietten geschnitten. Die Stoffservietten darin einrollen und beides mit einem weißen Bastband mehrfach umwickeln.

More grass for the serviettes. Blades of cat grass are flattened between sheets of laminating foil, which is then cut to size and rolled around the cloth serviettes. Several loops of raffia bast around the outside hold the roll tight.

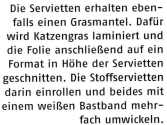

Niedrige Grasgarben mit Lilien. Ähnlich in der Gestaltung aber insgesamt niedriger und weniger streng wirkt diese Variante, bei der ebenfalls Gefäße mit Gras ummantelt werden. Beachtet werden sollte, dass die Gestaltung nach unten breiter wird und daher recht viel Platz auf dem Tisch beansprucht. Für eine optimale Wirkung dürfen die Bündel nicht zu dicht nebeneinander gestellt werden.

Low grass sheaths with lilies. Similar in design but altogether lower-slung and much less strict is this variant, which also features containers covered with grass. It should be noted that these creations have fairly big "feet", so they take up quite a bit of space on the table. For optimum impact the bundles shouldn't be placed too close together.

Im Gegensatz zur vorherigen Dekorationsvariante werden diesmal die Grasbündel genau anders herum um die Vasen gelegt, so dass das Gras an der Oberseite bündig abschließt und nach unten garbenartig ausfranst. Ein Streifen Walzblei verdeckt die Fixierung mit Haushaltsgummiband.

In contrast to the previous decoration variant, here the grass bundles are arranged around the vases the other way round, i.e. with the cut ends of the grass forming an even "rim" at the top and the growth ends radiating outwards like a fringe. A band of rolled metal conceals the rubber band mechanics.

Eine rechteckig gefaltete Serviette und das Besteck werden mit einem weißen Band zusammengehalten. Durch einen Plexiglaswürfel mit Loch wird ein Bündel Gras gesteckt und über das Band geschoben.

A serviette folded in a triangle and the cutlery are held together with a white ribbon. A bundle of grass is threaded through the hole in a Plexiglas cube and then slipped over the ribbon.

Plexiglaswürfel dienen als Tischkartenhalter. Zwei rechteckige Papierstücke werden laminiert, eines davon vorher mit dem Namen des Gastes beschriftet. Beide werden gelocht, mit einem schmalen, langen Band zusammengeknotet und zwischen die Gräser gesteckt.

Plexiglas cubes serve as place card holders. Two square pieces of paper are laminated, one of which bears the name of the guest. A hole is punched in each, a long ribbon is knotted through the holes and the finished card is wedged between the grass.

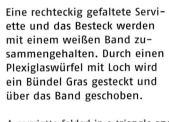

Zwiebelblüher

in bunter Gesellschaft

flowering bulbs

in colourful company

Blühende Frühlingszwiebeln. In den seltensten Fällen werden so genannte Weiße Feste auch mit einem weißen oder cremefarbenen Blumenschmuck für den Tisch gefeiert. Immer häufiger verlangen gerade jüngere Kunden, auch für solch klassische Anlässe, wie die Hochzeit, nach einer farbenfrohen und fröhlichen Dekoration. Im Frühling lässt sich diesem Wunsch am originellsten mit einer bunten Mischung aus Zwiebelblumen gerecht werden. Tulpen, Narzissen, Hyazinthen oder Iris erwecken Frühlingsgefühle und holen die so lang herbeigesehnte, zauberhafte Jahreszeit direkt auf die Hochzeitstafel. Der Clou an einer Dekoration mit Zwiebel- blühern: Die Blumen kommen samt ihrer Zwiebeln auf den Tisch. Das garantiert nicht nur erhöhte Aufmerksamkeit, sondern macht die Dekoration auch länger haltbar.

Flowering spring bulbs. Very seldom are the so-called "white ceremonies" decorated with either white or cream-coloured floral table decorations. More and more customers, especially the younger generation, are looking for gaily-coloured and cheery floral arrangements for such classic occasions as weddings. In spring this wish can be fulfilled in the most original way with a bright mix of bulbous plants. Tulips, daffodils, hyacinths or irises arouse spring feelings and deliver this much-cherished, magical season straight to the wedding table. The trick to decorations with bulbous plants: the flowers are served up on the table complete with their stems and bulbs. This will guarantee not only show-stopping attention but also longer-lasting table decorations.

Bunter Gläserfries im Zwiebellook. Unkompliziert in Wirkung und Herstellung ist dieser Tischschmuck, bei dem bunte Glasgefäße mit unterschiedlichen Zwiebelblumen gefüllt und in lockerer Reihung in der Tafelmitte platziert werden. Dabei sollten die Glasgefäße möglichst verschieden groß sein. Das sorgt zusätzlich für Spannung und Abwechslung.

Bright glass frieze in bulb look. Uncomplicated in design and quite easy to construct, this table decoration is a collection of coloured glass containers filled with assorted bulbous plants and arranged in a relaxed row along the centre of the table. For added rhythm and movement the glass containers should be of all different sizes.

Bevor die Zwiebeln in die Gläser gesetzt werden, sollten die Wurzeln von Erde befreit und ausgewaschen werden. Der verbleibende Raum in den Glasgefäßen wird mit Heidelbeergrün aufgefüllt.

Before the bulbs can be set in the glasses, the roots should first be rinsed and all bits of soil removed. The remaining space in the glass containers is filled in with blueberry branches.

Zwei Ringe aus Heidelbeergrün und Myrtendraht gewickelt sind ein symbolhaltiger wie dekorativer Serviettenschmuck. Eine herzförmige Perle wird mit einer Nadel fixiert und schmale, herabhängende Gimpe daran befestigt.

Two rings of blueberry greens bound with myrtle wire make not only a symbolic but also a decorative serviette adornment. A heart-shaped bead is attached with a pin and thin tails of gimp are tied to the heart.

Ein Kränzchen aus Heidelbeergrün ziert auch die Tischordnung. Ein Stück buntes Papier wird dafür mit den Namen der Gäste beschriftet und einfach auf einen kleinen Teller unter den Kranz gelegt.

A small wreath of blueberry foliage also adorns the list with the seating arrangement. The names of the guests are written on a piece of coloured paper and simply placed on a small plate under the wreath.

Zwiebelblumen sortenrein. Modern und klar wirkt diese Dekorationsvariante, bei der die Zwiebelblumen nach Sorten getrennt in niedrige, zylindrische Glasschalen eingestellt werden. Damit man die Zwiebeln auch erkennen kann, sollten die Gefäße möglichst aus ungefärbtem Glas sein. Die Zwiebeln werden vorher von Erde befreit und die Wurzeln ausgewaschen.

All sorts of bulbous plants. Modern and clear-cut is the effect of this decoration variant, which displays a jumble of flowering bulbs in straight-sided glass bowls. To make it easier for the guests to recognise all the flower varieties, choose bowls of clear glass. The bulbs are rinsed clean beforehand and all remnants of soil removed.

In den Gefäßen aus klarem Glas kommen nicht nur die Blüten, sondern auch die Zwiebeln gut zur Geltung. In die Schalen werden einige *Cornus*-Zweige eingestellt und die Zwiebelblumen dazwischen geklemmt.

In such containers of clear glass not only the flowers themselves but also their bulbs are shown off to advantage. A few *Cornus* twigs are first arranged in the containers and then the flowering bulbs are wedged between the twig mechanics.

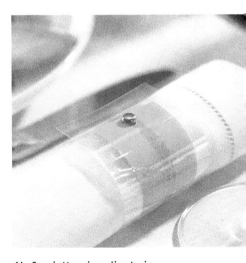

Kleine Tulpen in Mini-Glastöpfen werden zu originellen Tischkarten. Einer der *Cornus*-Zweige, die der Blumenzwiebel Halt geben, wird oben eingeritzt und ein laminiertes Namensschild daran festgeklemmt.

Miniature tulips in small glass pots are transformed into original place cards. One of the *Cornus* twigs supporting the bulb in the pot is promoted to card holder: It is slit open at the top and a laminated name tag is inserted in the slit.

Als Serviettenring dient ein bemaltes und laminiertes Stück Tonpapier, das gelocht, um die Serviette gerollt und mit einer Briefklemme zusammen geheftet wird.

The serviette ring is a hand-painted and laminated piece of construction paper with a hole punched in one side, is rolled around the serviette and fastened together with a paper clip.

Frühlingszwiebeln in Draht gesteckt. Die Frühlingsblumen mit ihren Zwiebeln in ein Geflecht aus buntem Draht zu klemmen, ist eine weitere Methode, den Blumen den nötigen Halt zu geben. Zu dieser unpreziösen Art der Blütenverarbeitung passen schlichte Zinkwannen, die hintereinander in der Mitte der Tafel platziert werden. Je nach Größe der Gästerunde kann diese Dekoration beliebig erweitert werden.

Spring bulbs with wire mechanics. Arranging spring flowers with their bulbs in a tangled web of coloured wire is another method for giving flowers the stability they need. Such a hodgepodge of flowers, stems and bulbs looks good in simple metal trays, placed in a row down the centre of the table. Depending on the number of guests, this decoration can be added to almost indefinitely.

Papageientulpen, kleine Narzissen und Mini-Iris machen die farbenfrohe Blütenmischung aus, die samt Zwiebeln im Drahtgeflecht verankert wird.

Parrot tulips, small narcissi and mini-irises comprise the gaily-coloured medley of flowers, which are all anchored with their bulbs in the wire structure.

Für die Dekoration werden Zwiebelblumen, farbiger Aludraht und Zinkwannen benötigt. Aus dem Aludraht ein Geflecht formen und in das Zinkgefäß einpassen.

For this table decoration you will need flowering spring bulbs, coloured aluminium wire and zinc trays. Mould the aluminium wire into a mesh the desired size and fit in the metal tray.

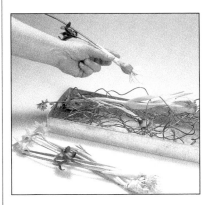

Die Blüten mit den Zwiebeln im Drahtgerüst verankern. So lange damit fortfahren, bis das Gefäß dicht und gleichmäßig gefüllt ist und der Draht kaum noch zu sehen ist.

The flowers are anchored with their bulbs in the wire grid. Keep on adding flowers until the container has a compact and balanced filling and until the wire is almost completely concealed.

Eine kleine quadratische Zink-wanne hält die Tischordnung parat und wird in gleicher Weise wie die großen Gefäße dekoriert. Auch die Servietten-ringe sind aus farbigem Aludraht geformt.

A small square zinc tray holds the seating arrangement in readiness and is decorated in the same way as the larger containers. The serviette rings are also moulded of coloured aluminium wire.

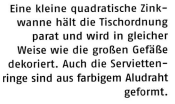

Glas an Glas
im zarten Blütenmix

glass to glass
with a delicate floral mix

Gläser für Transparenz und Leichtigkeit. Bei Festen, die mit Kindern in Zusammenhang stehen, wie z. B. Taufe, Kommunion oder Konfirmation, sollte der Tischschmuck möglichst leicht und natürlich wirken. Auch die Blütenauswahl sollte dem kindlichen Festanlass entsprechen. Alles gekünstelt oder zu gestylt Erscheinende wäre fehl am Platz. Die Verwendung von transparenten Glasgefäßen, in denen die Blumen auf verschiedene Art arrangiert werden können, ist eine Möglichkeit, um solch eine unbeschwerte Wirkung zu erreichen. Die Stiele der Blüten bleiben dabei sichtbar im Gefäß, vermitteln Leichtigkeit und Zartheit und bringen dennoch eine große Blütenvielfalt auf den Tisch. Wer dem Arrangement noch das i-Tüpfelchen aufsetzen und ihm zusätzlich Farbe verleihen möchte, gibt in die wassergefüllten Gläser ein paar Tropfen Aquarellfarbe.

Glass for transparency and lightness. At ceremonies involving children, such as christenings, first Holy Communion or confirmation, the table decorations should look as light and natural as possible. Even the choice of flowers should reflect the child-oriented meaning of the occasion. Anything too artificial or high-styled would be out of place here. Using transparent glasses of flowers in various arrangements is one way to achieve such light-hearted impact. The stems of the flowers remain in full view in the container, communicating lightness and tenderness despite the masses of florals assembled on the table. To add a finishing touch as well as an extra bit of colour, add a few drops of watercolour to the water in the glasses.

Blütenreigen als Kranz. Die lieblich-verspielte Gläserreihung in Kranzform eignet sich als dekorativer Tischschmuck für viele Anlässe. Bei einer Taufe erhält diese Gestaltungsform jedoch zusätzlich symbolische Bedeutung: Sie verkörpert den Kreislauf des Lebens mit seinen vielen Stationen, in den das Kind gerade erst eingetreten ist. Bei einer Hochzeit symbolisiert die Form Hoffnung, dass die Liebe des Paares niemals enden möge.

Ring around the rosy. The sweet and playful row of glasses arranged in a circle makes a lovely table decoration, suitable for many occasions. For a baptism this creative form takes on additional symbolic significance: It embodies the circle of life with all its many stops, into which the child has just entered. At a wedding the form symbolises the aspiring eternal love of the bride and groom.

Die Gläser werden auf einer runden, in der Farbe der Tischwäsche gestrichenen, Holzplatte kreisförmig angeordnet, mit gefärbtem Wasser und Blüten gefüllt. Einzelne Gräser sind durch die Blütenmischung gezogen und verbinden die Gläser miteinander.

The glasses are positioned in a ring around the outside edges of a round wooden board, painted to match the tablecloth, and are filled with coloured water and florals. A few blades of grass are intertwined around the assembly, connecting the glasses and adding rhythm.

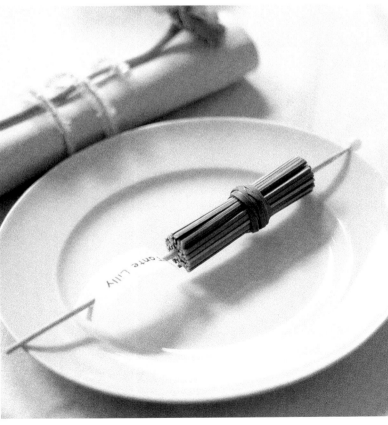

Für die Tischkarte wird ein Bündel Steelgras mit *Aristea africana* umwickelt und ein dünner Holzstab durchgesteckt. Ein Namensschild aus Papier wird gelocht, auf den Stab gezogen und das Stabende mit einer Perle beklebt.

For the place cards a bundle of steel grass is banded with *Aristea africana* and a thin wooden pick inserted through the middle. A paper name tag with a hole punched in one side is skewered on the pick. The tip of the stick is finished off with a bead.

Die gerollten Servietten umgeben Spiralen aus Stützdraht, der mit puscheligem Band umwickelt ist. Drahtanfang und -ende zieren jeweils eine Perle. Die Zinnienblüte wird einfach unter der Drahtspirale durchgezogen.

The rolled-up serviettes are encircled by spirals of stay wire, wound about with fluffy ribbon. Each end of the wire is adorned with a bead. The Zinnia flower is simply threaded through the wire spiral.

Blütengefüllte Gläser im Zentrum der Tafel. Wem der Blütenkranz der vorherigen Seite nicht üppig genug ist, kann in die Mitte des Kranzes weitere Gläser stellen und ebenfalls mit Blüten füllen. Übrigens: Beide Varianten lassen sich gut vorbereiten und zum Einsatzort transportieren, wenn man die Gläser mit Silikonmasse (aus dem Baumarkt) auf der Holz-platte fixiert. Vor Ort müssen dann nur noch Wasser und Blüten eingefüllt werden.

Centrepiece of flowers in glasses. If you find the floral wreath on the previous page too simple, you can add a few more glasses in the middle of the circle and fill them with flowers too. By the way: both alternatives are easier to construct and transport if the glasses are glued to the wooden board with silicone (DIY centre). Then all you have to do at the location is add the water and flowers.

Die fröhliche Blütenmischung
zieren zusätzlich kleine
Schnecken aus Rebenbindegarn.
Dazu wird das eine Ende in
eines der Gläser gestellt, das
andere zur Schnecke geformt.

The jolly mix of blooms is further
brightened by tiny snails of paper-
covered wire. One end of the
wire is anchored in one of the
glasses and the other coiled into
a snail shape.

Einen Drahtring mit Alchemilla
und Capsella *umwickeln. Eine
Schnecke aus Rebenbindegarn
formen und ein Band herab-
hängend daran befestigen.*

Wind a wire ring with Alchemilla
and Capsella. *Mould a snail of
paper-covered wire and attach
ribbon with long hanging tails.*

*An dem Kranz ein Reagenzglas
mit Draht befestigen und mit
Wasser füllen. Eine Rose in
das Glas stecken und daran die
Rebenbindegarn-Schnecke
befestigen.*

*Wire a glass tube to the wreath
and fill with water. Arrange a rose
in the glass and affix the wire snail
to the wreath.*

**Die Stuhllehnen schmücken
kleine Kränzchen mit einer
einzelnen Rosenblüte. Sofern
gewünscht, können daran auch
Platzkarten befestigt werden.**

The backs of the chairs are also
adorned by small wreaths, topped
by a single rose and a snail. If
desired, the place cards can also
be attached here.

Einzelne Gläser mit Filzblüten. Locker und ungezwungen sind hier die blütengefüllten Gläser in unregelmäßigem Abstand über den Tisch verteilt. Unter die echten Blumen haben sich einige Blüten aus Filz gemischt. An langem Aluminiumdraht, der um die Gläser gewickelt wird, scheinen sie fröhlich über der Tafel zu schweben.

Individual glasses with felt flowers. With loose and relaxed impact these flower-filled glasses wander over the surface of the table. Among the real flowers mingle a few felt impostors. Attached to long aluminium wires, one end wound around the glasses, they sway merrily over the table.

Die Tischkarte schmückt eine Zinnie im Reagenzglas, das mit Aluminiumdraht umwickelt und in einen kleinen Glastopf mit Perlenfüllung gestellt wird.

Each place card is adorned by a Zinnia in a glass tube with a coil of aluminium wire around it, standing in a small glass pot filled with beads.

Als Serviettenschmuck werden Steelgras und ein Zweig *Capsella* mit Draht umgewickelt und eine Filzblüte mit Perle daran befestigt.

As a serviette decoration *Xanthorrhoea australis* and a twig of *Capsella* are wound with wire and a felt flower is attached with a bead.

Cremefarbene Stumpenkerzen erhalten einen perlenbesetzten Kranz aus *Lunaria*-Blättern. Dafür werden die einzelnen Blätter mit Schmucknadeln im Kerzenwachs fixiert.

A cream-coloured pillar candle is adorned with a pearl-studded wreath of *Lunaria* leaves. The individual leaves are simply attached to the wax with beaded pins.

Kräuterduft
und Blütennostalgie

the scent of herbs
and floral nostalgia

Kräuter für alle Sinne. Vom Frühling bis tief in den Spätsommer bestechen Kräuter nicht nur Gaumen und Nase, sondern in Form von zauberhaften Sträußen und Gestecken auch das Auge. Wenn auf dem Teller die herrlichsten Gerichte ihren Kräuterduft entfalten, was läge da näher, als das grüne Kraut auch bei der Tischdekoration mit einzubeziehen? Vor allem die mediterranen Kräuter, wie Thymian, Rosmarin, Salbei und Lorbeer, bieten Floristen vielfältige Gestaltungsmöglichkeiten. Sie sind perfekte Begleiter für Blüten mit nostalgischem Charme, wie z. B. Rosen, kleine Nelken oder Wicken. In pastelligen Farben verbinden sich die Blumen mit dem frischen Kraut und verbreiten selbst im modernsten Ambiente eine Prise Landhausromantik.

Herbs for all the senses. From spring until well into late summer, fresh herbs not only tantalise the palate and nose, but are also a feast for the eyes in the form of enchanting bouquets and other floral assemblies. And if the most delicious dishes are unleashing herbal aromas on the table, what could be more logical than integrating these greens into the table decorations as well? Especially the Mediterranean herbs, such as thyme, rosemary, sage and bay, offer florists a host of creative possibilities. They make perfect escorts for flowers with nostalgic charm, such as roses, miniature carnations or sweet peas. In pastel shades the flowers blend in well with fresh herbs, and even in the most modern surroundings they spread a touch of country cottage romance.

Blütenpastell im Kräuterfries. Der Blütenfries auf Kräuterbasis schmückt lange Tafeln auf äußerst dekorative Weise. Als Unterlage dienen mehrere Steckschaumschalen, die mit Heißkleber auf einem Holzbrett hintereinander fixiert werden. Zuerst wird der Steckschaum mit *Tillandsia usneoides* abgedeckt, anschließend die Seiten mit Kräutern besteckt und die Blüten in der Mitte angeordnet.

Pastel flowers in a herbal frieze. A floral frieze based on herbs adorns long tables with extremely decorative impact. The assembly is based on several floral foam trays, which are hot-glued in a row to a wooden board. First the floral foam is based with *Tillandsia usneoides*, then the sides are based with herbs and the flowers are arranged in the centre.

Eine kleine Kräutertüte mit Rosenfüllung wird zum duftenden und romantischen Platzanweiser. Mit Band und einer Schmucknadel wird sie vorsichtig am Stuhl befestigt.

A tiny herby cone with a rose filling becomes a sweet-smelling, romantic place card. Suspended on a delicate ribbon it is carefully pinned to the back of the chair with a decorative pin.

Für die Platzanweiser Orchideenröhrchen mit Wasser füllen und mit Thymian und Schmuckdraht umwickeln. Als unteren Abschluss einen Glasanhänger am Draht befestigen.

For the place cards, orchid tubes are filled with water and wound about with thyme and decorative wire. The tip is finished off with a glass diamond on a wire.

Am kräuterumwickelten Orchideenröhrchen verschiedene Bänder sowie das Namensschild fixieren und eine Rose hineinstecken.

Tie a name tag to an orchid tube covered in herbs, add assorted ribbons and insert a single rose.

Die quadratisch gefalteten Servietten schmückt eine rosafarbene Nelke im gerollten *Galax*-Blatt. Floralkleber hält das Blatt zusammen, eine Schmucknadel fixiert die schmalen, herab fließenden Bänder.

The square-folded serviettes are adorned with a pink carnation in a rolled-up *Galax* leaf. Floral glue holds the leaf together, a decorative pin affixes the thin flowing ribbons.

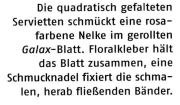

Amphoren für Kräuter und Blüten. Die antik anmutenden Gefäße in Amphorenform werden alle Liebhaber des gehobenen Landhausstils begeistern. Cremefarben und hochglänzend glasiert, harmonieren sie perfekt mit der pastelligen Kräuter-Blütenmischung. Für beschwingte Leichtigkeit sorgen die unterschiedlichen Größen der Gefäße.

Amphoras for herbs and flowers. Such antique-looking containers in the shape of amphoras will definitely catch the eye of lovers of country estate ambience. Cream-coloured and with a high gloss glaze, they harmonise perfectly with the pastel green medley of herbs. Use several different sized containers to add lightness and rhythm.

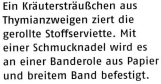

Die Gefäße sind alle mit Steckschaum gefüllt. Die größeren
werden zunächst mit einem
Kräuterrand, anschließend
mit den Blüten in der Gefäß-
mitte besteckt. Die kleineren
Amphoren erhalten eine einzelne Rosenblüte als Füllung.

The containers are all fitted with
floral foam. The larger ones are
first given a herbal border, and
then the flowers are arranged in
a dome in the centre. The smaller
amphoras hold only a single rose.

Ein Kräutersträußchen aus
Thymianzweigen ziert die
gerollte Stoffserviette. Mit
einer Schmucknadel wird es
an einer Banderole aus Papier
und breitem Band befestigt.

A herbal bouquet of thyme
sprigs adorns the rolled-up cloth
serviette. A decorative pin holds
a ring of paper and a wide ribbon
around it.

Die Tischkarten werden an
Thymiansträußchen befestigt
und an jeden Platz gelegt.
Breites Organzaband wird dazu
wie eine Manschette um das
Mini-Bouquet gewickelt und
mit schmalerem Band fixiert.

The place cards are attached to
tiny bouquets of thyme and laid at
each place. A broad collar of
organza ribbon is arranged around
the mini bouquet and a thinner
ribbon flows down from the
assembly.

Etageren mit Kräuterschmuck. Einen opulenten Gesamt-eindruck vermittelt diese Dekorationsvariante mit Etageren aus lackiertem Metall. Dabei ist der Arbeitsaufwand dieser Dekoration relativ gering. Kleine Gläser, die ursprünglich für Teelichter gedacht sind, werden jeweils mit Kräutern und einer einzelnen Blüte bestückt und auf den Etageren platziert. Am Griff der Etagere werden Bänder und goldene Drahtherzen befestigt.

Etagères with herby decorations. An opulent impression is made by this decoration variant with étagères of painted metal. And the time needed to make it is less than one would think. Small glasses, originally meant for tea lights, are filled with herbs and a single flower, and then grouped together on the shelves of the étagère. Ribbons and golden wire hearts hang from the handles of the ornamental stands.

Die schlichten, mehrdochtigen Kerzen werden auf Glasteller gesetzt und erhalten einen zierlichen Kranz aus Kräutern, glänzendem Draht und Schmucknadeln.

A simple multi-wick candle is set on a glass plate and adorned with a decorative wreath of herbs, shiny wire and beaded pins.

Für den Kerzenschmuck die Schmucknadeln über einer Flamme erhitzen und in gleich- mäßigem Abstand vorsichtig in die Kerze drücken.

To make the candle decoration, warm the pins over a flame and then push carefully into the base of the candle at regular intervals.

Verschiedene Kräuterzweiglein und Olivenblätter auf Schmuck- draht ziehen und mehrfach um die Kerze wickeln. Dabei den Draht immer wieder an den Schmucknadeln fixieren.

String sprigs of assorted herbs and olive leaves on decorative reel wire and wind several times around the candle. Tack the wire to the candle with beaded pins wherever necessary.

Handelsübliche Organza- säckchen sind mit frischen, duftenden Kräutern gefüllt. Die Namensschildchen werden mit schmalem Band daran befestigt.

Store-bought organza bags are filled with fresh scented herbs. The name tags are attached to the bags with tiny ribbons.

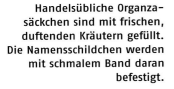

Blütenfülle

mit Schleierkraut

clustering

with baby's breath

Tausende kleiner, weißer Blüten. Die lieblichen kleinen Schleierkrautblüten wirken in der Menge und ihrer dichten Gestaltungsweise wie zuckersüße Sahnebaisers. Das macht sie zum idealen Schmuck für eine Kaffeetafel. Eine Dekoration, die sich auch für Kommunions- oder Konfirmationsfeiern eignet. Denn in ihrer außergewöhnlichen Optik spricht sie auch Kinder und Jugendliche an, die sich in der Regel weniger für Tischdekorationen begeistern lassen. Und schließlich sind sie an diesem Tag die Hauptpersonen. Aber auch für viele andere Anlässe ist Schleierkraut ein geeigneter Tischschmuck. Sofern es in entsprechend zeitgemäßer Form verarbeitet wird, kann es besonders festlich wirken und seinen Liebreiz spielerisch entfalten.

Thousands of tiny white flowers. The sweet little blooms of baby's breath, or *gypsophila*, when clustered together in a pavé arrangement, look like sugar-sweet meringues. This makes them ideal decorations for a tea party or coffee klatsch. A mouthwatering centrepiece that is excellently suited for a communion or confirmation party, as its unusual look will appeal to children of all ages – guests who otherwise don't pay much attention to the flowers on the table. And after all, a child is the most important person on this occasion. Baby's breath also makes an appropriate table decoration for many other kinds of parties. As long as it is integrated into up-to-the-minute designs, it can make a very festive impression and spread its charms in a playful way.

Verlockende Blütentorten. Diese Törtchen aus Schleierkraut und anderen weißen Blüten sind eine humorvolle Dekorationsidee für jede Kaffeerunde. Die Basis aus Steckschaum wird zunächst seitlich mit kleinen, angedrahteten Schleierkrautbündeln besteckt. Anschließend wird von oben die weiße Blütenmischung kuppelförmig in den Schaum gesteckt.

Tantalising floral cakes. These cakes of baby's breath and other white flowers are a humorous decoration idea for any tea party or coffee klatsch. The piece of floral foam is first based around the sides with tiny wired bundles of baby's breath. Then the other white flowers are arranged on the top of the foam in a dome shape.

Eine Margeritenblüte wird mit Schleierkraut umwickelt und ziert die Servietten. Das Ministräußchen kann, mit einem Namensschild versehen, auch als Tischkarte dienen.

A Marguerite daisy is wound about with baby's breath and adorns the serviettes. Add a name tag and the tiny bouquet can also serve as a place card.

Die langen Schleierkrautstängel bis auf wenige Zentimeter unter dem Blütenansatz kürzen. Das Schleierkraut mit silbernem Schmuckdraht auf einen stabilen Stützdraht wickeln.

Trim the long gypsophila stems back to just a few centimetres below the flower calyx. Wind around a heavy-gauge wire and affix with silver reel wire.

Den bewickelten Draht zum Kranz formen, die Enden miteinander verbinden und schmale Bänder herabfließend daran anbringen.

Bring the two ends of the wire together to form a wreath, bind the ends together and add thin ribbons with long tails.

Kleine Kränzchen aus Schleierkraut und langen Bändern sind eine liebevolle Ergänzung der Tischdekoration und schmücken die Stühle, auf denen die Gäste Platz nehmen.

Small wreaths of baby's breath and long ribbons are a loving supplement to the table decoration and adorn the chairs where the guests will sit.

Runde Blütengestecke. Etwas konventioneller und gefälliger wirkt die Verarbeitung des Schleierkrauts zu kleinen, runden Gestecken. Im Wechsel mit dicken Kerzen werden sie in einer Reihung auf dem Tisch platziert und wie kleine Törtchen auf dekorativen Tellern mit Fuß präsentiert. Ein breiter, farbiger Tischläufer unterstreicht die helle, freundliche Note der Dekoration.

Round floral assemblies. Somewhat more conventional and just as pleasing is gypsophila in small, round assemblies. Alternating with thick candles along the centre of the table, they are presented like little cakes on decorative plates with stands. A broad, coloured table runner underscores the bright, friendly effect of the decoration.

In Törtchenmanschetten gesetzte Baisers vom Bäcker werden zu originellen Tischkarten. Ein Band mit einer eingebundenen Margeritenblüte hält alles zusammen, die Namensfähnchen werden einfach in den Baiser gesteckt.

Meringues from the bakeshop set in fluted paper cups become original place cards. A ribbon tied around a Marguerite daisy holds everything together, the name flags are simply stuck in the meringue.

Eine runde Steckschaumunterlage mit Hilfe von Schmuckdraht mit Schleierkraut umwickeln, so dass die Blüten über den Rand des Steckschaumes deutlich hinausragen. Die Stiele und den Steckschaum mit breitem Band verdecken.

A round piece of floral foam is based with baby's breath and secured with decorative wire, so that the flowers clearly protrude over the edges of the foam. Conceal the stems and the foam with a wide ribbon.

Anschließend von oben die anderen Blüten kuppelförmig einstecken. Die Gestecke auf dekorative Glasteller setzen und in zwei Reihen versetzt auf dem Tisch anordnen.

Next arrange the other flowers in a dome shape on the top of the foam. Set the assemblies on decorative glass plates and place in two staggered rows along the table.

Die cremefarbenen Stumpenkerzen sind mit einem Band aus *Stachys*-Blättern verziert. Die Blätter werden schuppenartig mit Floralkleber zusammengeklebt und erst dann an den Kerzen befestigt. Die Kerzen auf flache Teller stellen und die verbleibende Fläche mit hellgrünem Granulat bestreuen.

The cream-coloured pillar candles are adorned with a band of *Stachys* leaves. The leaves are glued together in layers with floral glue and then attached to the candles. The candles are set on flat plates and the space around them strewn with pale green granulate.

Blütenfries mit Kerzen. Bei dieser Dekorationsvariante wird der Blütenschmuck zum funktionalen wie gleichermaßen dekorativen Kerzenständer. Dadurch bleibt die Tischgestaltung übersichtlich und auf der Tafel ist noch genug Platz für Geschirr und andere Dinge. Die langen Stabkerzen geben den flachen Gestecken Höhe und verleihen der Dekoration einen besonders festlichen Charakter.

Floral frieze with candles. In this decoration variant the floral centrepiece doubles as a decorative candleholder. This creates a clear and simple table decoration and leaves enough space on the table for the dishes and other objects. The long tapered candles add height to the flat design and lend the decoration a particularly festive character.

Als Basis der länglichen Gestecke dienen Steckschaumunterlagen mit Drahtgitter. Die Seiten werden zunächst mit *Tillandsia usneoides*, anschließend fest mit Schleierkraut umwickelt. Die Kerzen sind von oben zwischen die Gitter gesteckt und bekommen so den nötigen Halt. Zum Schluss werden die anderen Blüten von oben in den Steckschaum gesteckt.

The basis of these elongated assemblies is floral foam form covered with wire mesh. The sides are first based with *Tillandsia usneoides*, then tight clusters of baby's breath, secured with wire. The candles are inserted between the wires from the top and find the firm support they need. Ultimately, the other flowers are inserted in the foam from the top.

Ein Schleierkrautkissen ziert die Serviette und entsteht aus einem mit Kautschukband und Schleierkraut umwickelten Stück Pappe.

A *gypsophila* cushion adorns each serviette. These are made of a piece of card, wound about with baby's breath and secured with a rubber band.

So findet jeder Gast seinen Platz. Ein handelsüblicher Karten- oder Fotohalter dient zur Befestigung der Namensschildchen.

So that every guest finds their seat, name tags are clipped in standard commercial card or photo holders.

Rosenträume

für Romantiker

rosy dreams

for romantics

Rosen über Rosen. Rosen gelten allgemein als Dekorations-klassiker. Die Königin der Blumen besticht durch eine so große Sortenvielfalt, dass sie zu den beliebtesten Blumen überhaupt gehört. In feurigem Rot steht sie seit jeher für Liebe und Leidenschaft. In reinem Weiß gilt sie, der christ-lichen Symbolik zufolge, als Zeichen jungfräulicher Reinheit. Kein Wunder also, dass sie besonders gerne als Schmuck bei Hochzeiten und anderen „Weißen Festen" zum Einsatz kommt. Ob als Einzelblüte, als Strauß oder im Gesteck – obwohl man Rosen bereits in vielfältigsten Dekorations-variationen gesehen hat – es finden sich immer wieder neue Gestaltungsmöglichkeiten, die nicht nur ein Genuss für das Auge sind, sondern eine ganz eigene, symbolische Sprache sprechen.

Roses upon roses. Generally speaking, roses are considered to be decoration classics. The Queen of Flowers captivates everyone with her huge array of cultivars, making roses by far the most popular of all flowers. In fiery red the rose has always been a symbol of love and passion. In pure white roses are a Christian symbol of virginal purity. So it's no wonder that they are used so often in decorations for weddings and other "white ceremonies". Whether solo, in bouquets or arranged in assemblies – roses have been seen in all manner of decoration variations – there are always new creative possibilities being found for them. They are not only a feast for the eyes but also speak their own symbolic language.

Rosen im Glaspokal. Die Dekorationsvariante zeigt, wie sich Rosen auf ganz unkonventionelle und dennoch romantische Weise in Szene setzen lassen. Die Glasgefäße sind alle unterschiedlich gefüllt. Für die großen Pokale wird Steckschaum in den Gefäßen platziert und mit Schleierkraut und Rosen besteckt. Die kleinen Pokale sind mit einzelnen Rosen oder kleinen Stumpenkerzen gefüllt.

Roses in glass goblets. This decoration alternative shows how roses can be used in very unconventional and yet romantic designs. The glass containers are all filled with different floral fillings. The large goblets are fitted with floral foam that is based with baby's breath and roses. The smaller goblets are filled with single roses or small pillar candles.

Perlmuttfarbene Perlen sind für die sinnlichen Rosenblüten eine stilvolle Ergänzung. Die Rosen werden bis unter die Blüten-köpfe gekürzt und schwimmen auf den Perlen im Wasser.

A strand of mother-of-pearl beads makes a stylish escort for the sensual rose. The rose stem is cut just below the flower calyx and the flower is set afloat over the pearls in the water.

Für den Serviettenring werden Perlen auf einen Draht gefädelt, zum Ring geformt und über die gerollte Serviette geschoben. Die Schleife setzt einen farbigen Akzent.

For the serviette ring, beads are strung on a wire, which is bent to form a ring and slipped over the rolled-up serviette. The bow adds a colourful accent.

Als Namensschild dient ein Ständer aus Metall, an dem mit Draht ein Perlenkränzchen und das Namensschild befestigt werden. Die Rosenblüte wird auf den Ständer gespießt.

Small metal stands serve as name tags, adorned with tiny beaded wreaths on wires and name tags tied with tiny ribbons. The flower head of a rose is skewered on the top of the stand.

Rosen in Papiertüten. Auffällig und außergewöhnlich wirken die Rosen, wenn sie in selbstgeformten Tüten aus Tapetenbordüre präsentiert werden. Dem festlichen Anlass entsprechend sind die Blüten in hohe Sektfontänen gesteckt und zum Teil zusätzlich mit Schleierkrautkränzchen verziert. Beim Platzieren der Gläser sollte darauf geachtet werden, dass die Gäste noch guten Sichtkontakt zu einander haben und sich unterhalten können.

Roses in paper cones. Eye-catching and unusual are roses presented in handmade paper cones in glass champagne flutes, quite in keeping with the festive occasion. Some of the assemblies are additionally adorned with small gypsophila wreaths. The placement of the glasses should not disturb the guests or prevent them from seeing and conversing with one another.

Auch die Tischkarten sind an Rosen mit einer tütenartigen Papierumwicklung befestigt. Dafür wird das Namensschild mit einer Schmucknadel am Papier fixiert.

Smaller paper cones containing single roses serve as place cards. The name tag is attached to the paper with a beaded pin.

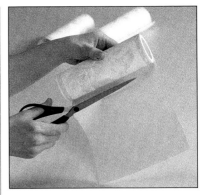

Zur Herstellung der Papiertüten eignet sich am besten Tapeten-bordüre mit einem zarten Muster. Mit der Schere ein ca. zwölf Zentimeter breites Stück von der Rolle abschneiden.

The best material for constructing these paper cones is strips of wall-paper border with a delicate floral pattern. With a pair of scissors cut a strip from the roll approximately twelve centimetres long.

Die gerollten Stoffservietten erhalten eine Banderole aus dem gleichen Papier wie die Rosentüten. Die Banderole wird an den Enden gelocht, ein schmales Satinband durch-gezogen und mit einer Schleife zusammengebunden.

The rolled-up cloth serviettes are given a band of the same paper as the rose cones. Holes are punched in the ends of the paper, a narrow satin ribbon threaded through the holes and tied in a bow.

Die Bordüre zur Tüte formen, so dass unten ein kleines Loch bleibt, durch das der Rosenstiel gesteckt werden kann. Am Rand mit Heiß-kleber fixieren. Beim Einstellen der Tüten in die Gläser darauf achten, dass nur der Stiel der Blüte im Wasser steht und das Papier nicht aufweicht.

Roll the border into a cone shape, leaving a small opening at the bot-tom for the rose stem to protrude. Secure along the edge with hot glue. When arranging the assemblies in the glasses be careful not to let the paper touch the water.

Private Feste

Geburtstag – Silberne Hochzeit – Goldene Hochzeit

Wenn im privaten Rahmen gefeiert wird, sind es vor allem die größeren Anlässe, für die ein Blumenschmuck beim Floristen geordert wird. Statt, wie sonst schon mal, selbst gestalterisch Hand anzulegen, wenden sich die meisten Gastgeber anlässlich von runden Geburtstagen, Goldener oder Silberner Hochzeit lieber vertrauensvoll an einen Fachmann. Für den Floristen gibt es bei der Dekoration derartiger Gelegenheiten keine speziellen Richtlinien. Ein Blumenschmuck mit persönlichem Bezug wird jedoch meistens als besonders gelungen empfunden. Dabei kann auf eigene Vorlieben der Gastgeber oder Jubilare eingegangen oder in der Gestaltung mit originellen Accessoires individuell Bezug auf den Anlass der Feier genommen werden. In jedem Fall sollte bei Farb- und Blumenauswahl auch der Ort, an dem gefeiert wird, Berücksichtigung finden. Ob im schlichten, modernen Restaurant oder im plüschigen, privaten Ambiente – hier sind Stilbewusstsein und Einfühlungsvermögen des Floristen besonders gefragt.

When parties are given in a private sphere, it has to be a major occasion if the buffet or table arrangements are ordered from a florist. Rather than trying their own hand at doing the flowers as usual, the hostesses of such affairs as important birthday parties and golden or silver anniversary celebrations are usually glad to rely on a professional for their flowers. For the florist there are no special guidelines for decorations for such special events. Floral arrangements with a personal theme, however, are always popular. A short consulting session with the customer will suffice for discussing any personal preferences or the possible integration of original accessories related to the guest of honour or the theme of the occasion. In any case, the colour scheme and choice of flowers should also take into consideration the setting or room in which the party is to take place. Whether in a simple, modern restaurant or in a cosy, private atmosphere – here again the style consciousness and intuition of the florist will be put to the test.

private parties

birthday – silver anniversary – golden anniversary

Calluna

mit Silberglanz

calluna

with silver shine

Hunderte kleiner Blüten für den Ehrentag. Im Spätsommer überzieht das niedrigwüchsige Heidekraut in der freien Natur ganze Landstriche mit einem leuchtenden, pinkfarbenen Blütenteppich. Als Topfpflanzen sind Callunen und Eriken spätestens ab September in den meisten Gärtnereien erhältlich. Von dort aus nehmen sie ihren Weg auf herbstliche Balkone und Terrassen, aber auch als Zimmerpflanzen werden Calluna und Co. immer beliebter. Warum sollten also die weiß über rosa bis hin zu leuchtend pink blühenden Pflanzen nicht auch als Tischdekoration ihren Reiz ausspielen dürfen? Noch dazu, wo sie als Symbol für Glück, Heim und Familie gelten. In der Verarbeitung sind die Blüten völlig unkompliziert und dabei äußerst wandlungsfähig, wie die folgenden Dekorationsvarianten zeigen.

Hundreds of tiny blossoms for the special day. In late summer, low wide-spreading heather plants carpet large areas of open countryside in luminous shades of pink. As pot plants, heather and erica are available in most garden centres at the latest from September onwards. From there they make their way to autumn balconies and terraces, although Calluna and Co. are also enjoying resurgent popularity as house plants. So why shouldn't these flowering plants in shades ranging from white to rose to brilliant pink and purple be allowed to display their charms as a table decoration? Plus, heather is a symbol of good fortune, home and family. These plants are very uncomplicated to work with and also extremely versatile, as the following decoration ideas show.

Calluna als blühender Rahmen. Wer traditionelle Formen bevorzugt, für den sind Blütenfriese die passende Dekoration. Erfrischend anders ist ihre Wirkung, wenn sie statt in der Tischmitte längs zwischen den Gedecken platziert werden. *Calluna* bildet den leuchtenden Rahmen für eine gesteckte, spätsommerliche Blütenmischung. Mit Schlagmetall versilberte *Senecio*-Blätter veredeln den Schmuck und verweisen dezent auf den Anlass einer Silberhochzeit.

Calluna as a flowering frame. For those who prefer traditional shapes, floral friezes are right on the mark for table decorations. The effect will be refreshingly different if, instead of being placed along the centre of the table, the friezes are arranged between the place settings. *Calluna* forms the vibrant frame for a foam-based, late-summer mix of flowers. *Senecio* leaves shining with a coat of silver leaf add an elegant touch and remind the guests discreetly that the occasion is a silver wedding anniversary.

Ein schmales Kränzchen aus *Calluna* ziert die weißen Stumpenkerzen in formschönen Gläsern. Eine einzelne, weiße Strohblumenblüte ist mit einer Schmucknadel daran befestigt.

A thin wreath of *Calluna* adorns the white pillar candle in a lovely-shaped glass. A single white straw-flower is pinned to the wreath with a beaded pin.

Für die Rahmen der Blütenfriese kleine Callunenbündel mit Draht zusammenfassen. Für die weitere Verarbeitung werden Schmucknadeln und pro Gesteck ein länglicher Steckschaumblock mit Unterlage benötigt.

For the frame of the floral frieze, tie small bundles of Calluna and secure with wire. All further work will be done with decorative pins, and one longesh block of floral foam on a tray per assembly.

Die Callunenbündel mit je einer Schmucknadel im Steckschaum fixieren bis der Rand vollständig bedeckt ist. Anschließend von oben die Blütenmischung stecken.

Pin the Calluna bundles around the outside of the floral foam until all the edges are completely covered. Then arrange the flowers from the top, pushing the stems firmly into the foam.

Rosafarbenes Tonpapier trägt den Namen des jeweiligen Gastes. Darauf ein Callunenbündel, das mit einer Schmucknadel an der Serviette festgesteckt wird.

Squares of pink construction paper sport the names of each guest. On top of the paper lies a bunch of *Calluna*, attached to the serviette with a beaded pin.

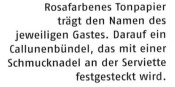

Herzenssache für Calluna. Romantiker wird dieser Dekorationsvorschlag begeistern, der sich in seiner Gestaltungsart besonders für Silberhochzeiten und andere Herzensangelegenheiten eignet. *Calluna* wird dafür mit silbernem Schmuckdraht auf herzförmige Strohunterlagen gewickelt. Eine Dekoration, die auch ohne Wasserversorgung lange frisch bleibt und anschließend einfach eintrocknen kann.

Calluna affair of the heart. Those who are romantic at heart will love this decoration idea, which is particularly well-suited for a silver wedding anniversary and other such affairs of the heart. A heart-shaped straw base is covered with *Calluna* and wrapped with silver reel wire. A decoration that will stay fresh without water for a long time and which can be allowed to dry.

Kleine Callunenkränzchen mit angedrahteten Perlen werden zum lieblichen Schmuck für Teelichter, die auf hohen Glasleuchtern über der Tafel thronen.

Tiny *Calluna* wreaths with beads swinging on perpendicular wires around them make sweet decorations for tea lights, presiding over the table scenery on tall glass candleholders.

Besteck und Serviette fasst eine Banderole aus breitem Samtband zusammen. Über die Nahtstelle wird ein mit Schlagmetall versilbertes Herz aus Pappe geklebt.

Cutlery and serviette are held together by a broad band of velvet ribbon. A cardboard heart covered in silver leaf is glued over the seam in the ribbon.

Die Sitzordnung für jeden Tisch entnehmen die Gäste rosafarbenem Tonpapier, das mit einer Schmucknadel an einem Callunenherz festgesteckt wurde.

The seating arrangement for every table is written on a pink square of construction paper, which is pinned to a *Calluna* heart with a beaded pin.

Buchsbaum

im Goldrausch

boxwood

in gold fever

Goldenes Jubiläum mit Buxus. Ein ganz besonderer Anlass für eine große Feier mit Familie und Freunden ist die Goldene Hochzeit eines Paares. Da darf die Farbe Gold auch bei der Dekoration eine tragende Rolle spielen. In Form von Accessoires und Geschirr verbreitet sie Glanz auf der Tafel. Goldgelbe Blüten und Beeren unterstreichen den strahlenden und sonnig-warmen Charakter der Dekoration. Doch damit so viel Glanz perfekt zur Geltung kommt, braucht er optisch einen beruhigenden Gegenpol. Buchsbaum ist dafür ein ansprechender und noch dazu symbolträchtiger Begleiter. Von jeher galten seine immergrünen Zweige als Zeichen der Treue und immerwährenden Liebe. In Kranzform gebunden und mit zarten Bändern geschmückt, schwebt er an langen Stäben über der goldenen Tafel und gibt den blumigen Gestecken einen passenden Rahmen.

Golden anniversary with box. A very special occasion for a big celebration with family and friends is the golden wedding anniversary of a couple. Table decorations with a monochromatic colour scheme in gold hues play a supporting role here. In the form of accessories and tableware, a golden sheen spreads over the entire table. Golden-yellow flowers and berries further underscore the brilliant and warm sunny character of the table decorations. However, a bit of contrast is necessary to show off so much gilt to advantage perfectly. Boxwood is the ideal choice here: not only attractive in a classic way but also a suitable escort full of symbolism. Its evergreen sprigs have always been considered a symbol of loyalty and everlasting love. Intertwined in wreath shapes and adorned with delicate, flowing ribbons it sways on long poles over the golden table, providing the floral assemblies with a fitting framework.

Goldgelber Blütenmix im Topf. Die mit Blüten besteckten Töpfe sind schnell angefertigt, lassen sich gut vorbereiten und wirken trotzdem sehr festlich. Als Basis im Topf dient Steckschaum, in den zunächst die Buchsbaumzweige kranzförmig gesteckt werden. Die weitere Füllung variiert und besteht mal aus einer einzigen Blütensorte, mal aus einer goldgelben Blüten- und Beerenmischung.

Golden floral compositions in pots. These foam-based pot assemblies are quick and easy to make, can be done up in advance and yet have very festive impact. The pots are fitted with floral foam and the box twigs are first arranged in a ring around the rim. The floral filling varies: Some of the pots have a single bloom, some a single variety tightly massed, and some a combination of yellow and gold flowers and berries in analogous colour harmony.

Kleine, goldene Bilderrahmen zeigen das Jubelpaar an seinem 50 Jahre zurückliegenden Festtag und sind eine nette Erinnerung. Auch die Menüfolge kann in goldenen Rahmen präsentiert werden.

Small gilded picture frames show the couple on their wedding day 50 years ago and make nice keepsakes for the guests. Similarly, the menu can be displayed in a gilded frame.

Als Tischkarten dienen kleine Kränzchen aus Zieräpfeln, die auf Steckdraht gefädelt werden. Einer der Äpfel ist mit Schlagmetall vergoldet. Das Namensschild wird mit Band am Kranz befestigt.

The place cards are tiny wreaths of ornamental apples, strung on pieces of stub wire. One of the apples in each is gilded with gold leaf. The name tag is attached to the wreath with a flowing piece of ribbon.

Für kleinere Töpfe reicht eine einzelne Sonnenblume mit Buchsbaum als Füllung aus. Gerade die Unterschiedlichkeit der Gestecke macht den Charme der Dekoration aus.

For smaller pots a single sunflower encircled by a ring of box is enough. The combination of pots with their medley of fillings is what makes this table decoration so charming.

Goldener Blütenfries. Etwas konventioneller und traditionel-
ler wirkt die goldgelbe Blütenmischung, wenn sie als großer
Fries gesteckt und in der Mitte des Tisches platziert wird.
Die Schmalseiten des Gesteckes schmücken Schleifen, deren
Bandenden sich lang auf der Tafel ausbreiten. Zwei auf den
Blüten liegende, goldene Drahtringe symbolisieren die
Eheringe des Goldpaares.

Golden floral frieze. Somewhat more conventional and traditional
is a similar combination of gold and yellow florals in the form of a
long frieze running down the centre of the table. The ends of the
assembly are adorned with ribbons with long tails trailing down
the length of the table. Two rings of gold wire lying on top of the
flowers symbolise the wedding bands of the golden couple.

Blüten und Buchsbaumrahmen sind in Steckschaumziegel gesteckt. Als Gefäß dient ein flacher Terrakotta-Untersetzer, der mit Schlagmetall vergoldet wird.

The flowers and box twigs are based on a brick of floral foam, placed on a flat terracotta tray, which is covered in a layer of gold leaf.

Kleine, mit Schlagmetall vergoldete Tontöpfe dienen als Kerzenhalter und Tischkarten. Sie werden mit Moos gefüllt und entweder ein Teelicht oder ein Zierapfel mit dem Namensschild darauf gesetzt.

Small gilded clay pots serve as candleholders and place cards. They are filled with moss and hold either a tea light or an ornamental apple bearing a name flag.

Auch die Serviettenringe sind selbst gemacht. Dafür werden hölzerne Gardinenringe mit Schlagmetall und Sprühkleber vergoldet.

The serviette rings are also handmade. Simple wooden curtain rings are gilded with gold leaf, patted on with spray adhesive.

Wolfgang

Blütenmix

in Frühlingslaune

floral mix

in spring fever

Der Frühling in bunter Gesellschaft. Private Anlässe, wie beispielsweise Geburtstage, werden häufig etwas legerer gefeiert. Wie seriös, ungezwungen oder unkonventionell eine Feier gerät, hängt dabei sicherlich nicht nur vom Ambiente, sondern auch vom Alter und Lebensumfeld der Gastgeber und Gäste ab. So kann beispielsweise die Dekoration für eine Feier im Freundeskreis der Mitdreißiger ebenso bunt und unkompliziert ausfallen, wie die allgemeine Atmosphäre und Stimmung der Party. Eine farbenfrohe Frühlingsblütenmischung in schlichten Zinkgefäßen wird in dieser Gästerunde gut ankommen und dem Anlass sicherlich gerecht. Dabei müssen keine besonders edlen Blüten verwendet werden, denn nicht die einzelne Blume, sondern die Gesamtwirkung zählt bei dieser Dekoidee.

Springtime in colourful company. Private celebrations, for example birthday parties, are often celebrated less formally. Just how serious, casual or unconventional a party is will not only depend on the atmosphere but also on the age and lifestyles of the hosts and their guests. For example the table decorations for a bash with friends in their thirties can be just as colourful and uncomplicated as the general atmosphere and mood of the party itself. A gaily-coloured mix of spring flowers in simple metal containers is just the ticket for such a group of guests on this occasion. The flowers needn't be exotic or expensive, as the impact in this deco idea is created by the overall effect and not the individual flower.

Blütenrunde mit Spiegelbild. Die kreisförmige Anordnung der blütengefüllten Gefäße eignet sich besonders für große runde oder quadratische Tische. Auf originelle Weise verdoppelt sich hier die Blütenzahl, denn die Zinkgefäße sind auf dem Rand eines runden Spiegels platziert. Einige Typha-Grashalme werden durch die Blütenmischung gezogen und verbinden die einzelnen Gefäße miteinander.

Mirrored floral ring. A circular arrangement of flower-filled pots is especially well-suited for large round or square tables. In an original way the number of flowers is doubled, as the zinc containers are placed around the rim of a round mirror. A few blades of Typha grass are threaded through the floral composition and connect the individual pots.

Schlichte Zinkgefäße betonen den unkomplizierten Charakter der Dekoration. Als Füllung eignen sich bunte Frühlings- blumen wie Tulpen, Narzissen Anemonen, Ranunkeln und viele mehr.

Simple metal pots emphasise the uncomplicated character of the table decorations. Almost any kind of bright spring flowers, such as tulips, daffodils, anemones or buttercups, can be used as filling for the pots.

Fröhlich bunte Akzente setzen farbige Kunststoffblüten. Mit Hilfe von Draht werden sie zu dekorativen Serviettenringen. Einfarbiges schmales Band wird als zusätzlicher Schmuck einfach angeknotet.

Colourful silk flowers add bright cheery accents. Strung on a wire they are transformed into a decorative serviette ring. Mono- chromatic narrow ribbons are simply knotted to the rings for a finishing touch.

Für die Tischkarten werden aus aufgerolltem Typha-Gras kleine Ringe geformt und mit einer gekürzten Schmucknadel mit Filzblümchen zusammengefasst. Von hinten eine Perle dagegen stecken und mit Klebstoff befes- tigen. Auch das Namensschild wird durch die Nadel fixiert.

For the place cards a strip of Typha grass is rolled into a small ring and pinned together with a felt flower; behind the flower another bead is glued. The name tag is also held in place by the pin.

Bunte Topfparade. Für längere Tafeln eignet sich eine Dekoration aus einzelnen Zinkgefäßen, die zu einem langen Fries in der Tischmitte arrangiert werden. Statt die Gefäße komplett mit Blüten zu füllen, werden sie mit kurzgeschnittenen Heidelbeer-, Birken- und *Cornus*-Zweigen besteckt und die Blüten darin eingeklemmt. So wird mit weniger teurem Werkstoff eine ebenso schöne Wirkung erzielt.

Brilliant pot parade. For longer tables a decoration made of individual zinc containers arranged in a long frieze down the centre of the table is well-suited. Rather than filling the pots completely with flowers they are first stuffed with chopped blueberry, birch and *Cornus* twigs and then only a few blooms are wedged in the spaces between the sticks. This way, the same impact can be achieved with far less of the more expensive materials.

Für den bunten Topf-Blüten-Fries können ruhig unterschied-lich hohe Gefäße verwendet werden. Das bringt Abwechslung und macht die Dekoration spannender. In die kleinsten Gefäße lassen sich niedrige Kerzen einsetzen.

For a colourful pot-and-flower frieze the containers can be different sizes. This adds diversity and rhythm to the table decora-tions. In the smallest pots votive candles add tiny highlights.

Einer der Zinktöpfe wird mit Pomponband umwickelt und dient als dekorativer Besteckhalter, aus dem sich die Gäste selbst bedienen können. Das Reagenzglas mit Narzissenfüllung ist mit einem Gardinenklip am Rand des Gefäßes fixiert.

Pom-pom ribbon is looped around the rim of one of the zinc contai-ners and serves as a decorative cutlery dispenser, from which the guests can help themselves. The glass tube filled with narcissus is attached to the rim of the pot with a curtain clip.

Kleine Zinktöpfe, mit *Euphorbia spinosa* und Tête-à-Tête-Narzissen gefüllt, dienen als liebliche Tischkarten. Buntes Tonpapier wird mit den Namen der Gäste beschriftet und einfach an den Topf geklebt.

Small zinc containers filled with *Euphorbia spinosa* and miniature tête-à-tête daffodils serve as pretty place cards. The names of the guests are written on strips of coloured construction paper, which are simply glued to the sides of the pots like labels.

Blütenpracht
im Herbstgewand

floral splendour
in autumn dress

Herbstliches Blütenpotpourri. Der Herbst bietet eine Blüten-, Beeren- und Blättervielfalt, die kaum zu überbieten ist. In den schönsten Farben leuchten Aster, Dahlie, Chrysantheme, Erika, *Calluna* und viele, viele mehr in den Gärten um die Wette. Diese relativ robusten Blumen eignen sich besonders für rustikalere und gediegenere Dekorationen und treffen damit häufig den Geschmack der Generation 50 plus. Dabei kann die Gesamtwirkung der Dekoration je nach Kombination und Art der Blütenverarbeitung stark variieren. Werden die traditionellen Herbstblüten in weniger traditioneller und außergewöhnlicher Form verarbeitet, erfreuen sie sich dagegen auch bei den Jüngeren großer Beliebtheit.

Autumn potpourri of flowers. Autumn offers a huge diversity of flowers, berries and leaves that is hard to top. In the most beautiful colour shades, asters, dahlias, chrysanthemums, erica, *Calluna* and lots of others light up gardens everywhere. These relatively hardy flowers are especially well-suited for more rustic and tasteful decorations and appeal especially to the over-50 crowd. At the same time the look of the table decorations can greatly vary, depending on the combination and style of the floral design. And if these traditional fall flowers are used in less traditional and more unusual designs they will also be a hit with the younger generation.

Herbstvielfalt in Blütentüten. Modern und unkonventionell wird hier mit den traditionellen Herbstblühern umgegangen. Langstielige Astern, Dahlien und Hagebutten werden mit *Calluna* und Schmuckdraht umwickelt, so dass dabei tüten-ähnliche Formen entstehen. Dabei können mal einzelne Blüten, mal mehrere zusammen ummantelt werden. In schlichten, hohen Glasvasen werden sie in lockerer Reihung auf dem Tisch angeordnet.

Autumn diversity in floral cones. Here our traditional fall flowers are done up in a really modern and unconventional way. Long-stemmed asters, dahlias and rose hips are wrapped in bundles of *Calluna* and moulded into cone shapes with reel wire. Either single flowers or small bouquets can be encircled this way. Placed in tall, straight glass vases they are arranged in a loose row down the centre of the table.

Auch die Tischkarte wird im Tütenformat gestaltet. In einen kleinen Holzwürfel wird mit Hilfe eines Akkubohrers ein Loch gebohrt und ein Splitstab darin fixiert. Die mit *Calluna* umwickelte Hagebutte wird darauf gespießt und das Namensschild mit einer Schmucknadel festgesteckt.

Even the place cards are cone-shaped. A hole is drilled in the top of a small wooden cube with a cordless drill and a wooden pick is anchored in the hole. A single rosehip is wrapped in *Calluna* and skewered on the stick; the name tag is attached with a beaded pin.

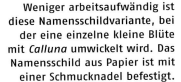

Guido

Für die tütenförmige Dekoidee werden Herbstblumen, Blüten-rispen von mehreren Calluna-Pflanzen und Schmuckdraht benötigt. Die Stiele der Blüten entweder einzeln mit Calluna umwickeln oder zu mehreren zusammenfassen.

For the cone-shaped deco idea you will need autumn flowers, the flow-ering panicles of several heather plants and decorative reel wire. The stems of the flowers are either wrapped in Calluna individually or in small bunches.

Mit der Umwicklung am Blüten-kopf beginnen. Dabei die Calluna so anlegen, dass sie oben etwa bündig mit der Blüte abschließt. Die Umwicklung nach unten fortführen, das Stielende unbe-deckt lassen.

Start by wrapping the flower head. One frond at a time, arrange Calluna around the flower with the tips level with the top of the flower. Wrap with wire, working down the stem of the flower until it is completely covered.

Weniger arbeitsaufwändig ist diese Namensschildvariante, bei der eine einzelne kleine Blüte mit *Calluna* umwickelt wird. Das Namensschild aus Papier ist mit einer Schmucknadel befestigt.

For a name tag version that is quicker and easier to make: wrap a single flower in a bundle of *Calluna*. The paper name tag is attached with a beaded pin.

Bettina

Herbstvielfalt im Häkelfries. Konventioneller wirkt die Herbstblütenmischung in der Verarbeitung zum langen Fries. Erst auf den zweiten Blick erschließt sich dem Betrachter die außergewöhnliche Technik, in der hier die Blüten gesteckt sind. Denn als Basis dient ein Häkelgerüst aus Rebenbinde-garn, in das die Blüten und Beeren eingearbeitet werden.

Autumn diversity in a crocheted frieze. For a more conventional table decoration a medley of autumn flowers is arranged in a long frieze. Only upon second glance will the observer notice the extra-ordinary mechanics here: The flowers and berries are arranged in a crocheted grid of paper-covered wire.

Für diese Art der Dekoration eignen sich fast alle Herbstblüten. Allerdings sollte bei der Auswahl darauf geachtet werden, dass die Blüten genug Leuchtkraft haben und den Tischschmuck zum Strahlen bringen.

For this type of decoration almost every kind of autumn flower can be used. However, the brightest and most luminous varieties should be selected for a striking centerpiece in autumn hues.

Orchideenröhrchen werden mit *Calluna* umwickelt und bieten den Blüten die nötige Wasserversorgung. So geschmückt werden sie kreuz und quer in das Häkelgerüst eingeklemmt. Beeren, Efeublätter und *Clematis*-Fruchtstände sind einfach dazwischen gesteckt.

Orchid tubes are covered in *Calluna* and integrated in the arrangement to supply the flowers with water. Thus adorned, they can be inserted wherever necessary in the crocheted structure. Berries, ivy leaves and *Clematis* infructescence are simply arranged in the spaces.

Die gerollten Stoffservietten erhalten einen Ring aus grob gehäkeltem Rebenbindegarn. Eine einzelne *Gomphrena*-Blüte wird als blühender Akzent darunter geklemmt. Je nach Geschmack kann die Blüte von Gedeck zu Gedeck variieren.

The rolled-up cloth serviette is held together by a ring of loosely crocheted twine. A single *Gomphrena* is tucked under this band as an extra highlight. Depending on personal taste, the serviette flower can vary from one place setting to the next.

Werkstoffe – Materialien – Hersteller

(Alle nicht näher bezeichneten Produkte und Materialien sind im Floristikgroßhandel erhältlich.)

botanicals – materials – sources

(All products and materials not specifically listed are available at florists' supply wholesalers.)

Feste im Freien
outdoor parties

Seite 8–15

Humulus lupulus, Dahlia, Setaria italica, Panicum capillare, Rosa multiflora, Physalis alkekengi

Filzband (Hey-Sign)

Page 8-15

Humulus lupulus, Dahlia, Setaria italica, Panicum capillare, Rosa multiflora, Physalis alkekengi

felt band (Hey-Sign)

Seite 16–23

Rosa Cultivar, Diascia Cultivar, Helichrysum bracteatum, Anthriscus caucalis, Lathyrus odoratus, Muehlenbeckia, Geranium, Verbena Cultivar, Rosa multiflora, Viburnum lantana

Schnapsgläser (Metro), Zinkwannen (Klocke)

Page 16-23

Rosa cultivar, Diascia cultivar, Helichrysum bracteatum, Anthriscus caucalis, Lathyrus odoratus, Muehlenbeckia, Geranium, Verbena cultivar, Rosa multiflora, Viburnum lantana

schnapps glasses (Metro), zinc trays (Klocke)

Seite 24–31

Fallopia japonica, Gerbera Cultivar, Seteria italica, Panicum capillare, Rosa Cultivar, Rosa multiflora, Dahlia, Aster, Anthriscus caucalis, Lysimachia, Matricaria recutita, Leucanthemum vulgare, Jasminum, Nigella damascena

Page 24-31

Fallopia japonica, Gerbera cultivar, Seteria italica, Panicum capillare, Rosa cultivar, Rosa multiflora, Dahlia, Aster, Anthriscus caucalis, Lysimachia, Matricaria recutita, Leucanthemum vulgare, Jasminum, Nigella damascena

Offizielle Anlässe
official occasions

Seite 34–39

Phalaenopsis, Paphiopedilum, Leucospermum truncatulum, Schinus terebinthifolius, Tillandsia usneoides, Stachys byzantina

Band (Goldina); Vasen (Sandra Rich); Teelichtgläser (Boltze)

Page 34-39

Phalaenopsis, Paphiopedilum, Leucospermum truncatulum, Schinus terebinthifolius, Tillandsia usneoides, Stachys byzantina

ribbon (Goldina); vases (Sandra Rich); tea light glasses (Boltze)

Seite 40–45

Triticum aestivum, Dahlia, Rosa Cultivar, Heuchera americana, Dendranthema, Hypericum, Malus sylvestris, Lysimachia, Deschampsia cespitosa

Vasen (Sandra Rich)

Page 40-45

Triticum aestivum, Dahlia, Rosa cultivar, Heuchera americana, Dendranthema, Hypericum, Malus sylvestris, Lysimachia, Deschampsia cespitosa

vases (Sandra Rich)

Seite 46–53

Papaver nudicaule, Tulipa, Anemone, Ranunculus asiaticus, Clivia miniata, Heuchera, Euphorbia spinosa, Xanthorrhoea australis

Glasgefäße, Teelichtgläser (Klocke); Drahtgefäße (1.2.3 Floral Ideen); Teller (Ikea); eckige Schalen auf Teller (ASA); Kerzen (Arte); Schmuckdraht (Buco); gelochtes Band (Goldina); Schmucknadeln (Zemlin), Filzblumen (Halbach)

Page 46-53

Papaver nudicaule, Tulipa, Anemone, Ranunculus asiaticus, Clivia miniata, Heuchera, Euphorbia spinosa, Xanthorrhoea australis

glass containers, tea light glasses (Klocke); wire containers (1.2.3 Floral Ideen); plate (Ikea); square dishes on plates (ASA); candles (Arte); decorative reel wire (Buco); ribbon with holes (Goldina); decorative pins (Zemlin), felt flowers (Halbach)

Seite 54–59

Anemone, Tulipa, Iris latifolia, Aspidistra elatior, Hedera helix, Xanthorrhoea australis

Kerzen (Molca); Bastband (Halbach); Teller, Kartenhalter (Ikea); Büroklemme (Bösner)

Page 54-59

Anemone, Tulipa, Iris latifolia, Aspidistra elatior, Hedera helix, Xanthorrhoea australis

candles (Molca); bast (Halbach); plate, cardholder (Ikea); paper clips (Bösner)

Seite 60–67

Poa annua, Lolium perenne, Allium giganteum, Campanula glomerata, Campanula persicifolia, Leucanthemum superbum, Leucanthemum vulgare, Matricaria recutita, Ageratum houstonianum, Lathyrus odoratus, Veronica spicata, Aquilegia vulgaris, Nigella damascena, Anethum graveolens, Anthriscus sylvestris, Hydrangea macrophylla

Satinband (Senn); Wassergläser (Ikea); Tischläufer, Servietten (Klocke), grüne quadratische Teller (ASA); längliche Gesteckschalen, Kranzunterlagen (Oasis)

Page 60-67

Poa annua, Lolium perenne, Allium giganteum, Campanula glomerata, Campanula persicifolia, Leucanthemum superbum, Leucanthemum vulgare, Matricaria recutita, Ageratum houstonianum, Lathyrus odoratus, Veronica spicata, Aquilegia vulgaris, Nigella damascena, Anethum graveolens, Anthriscus sylvestris, Hydrangea macrophylla

satin ribbon (Senn); water glasses (Ikea); table runner, serviettes (Klocke), green square plate (ASA); long tray, floral foam base (Oasis)

Weiße Feste
white ceremonies

Seite 70–77

Eustoma grandiflorum, Rosa Cultivar, Paeonia lactiflora, Alstroemeria ligtu, Pulsatilla vulgaris, Viburnum opulus, Clematis, Alchemilla mollis, Lathyrus odoratus, Ornithogalum arabicum, Galax urceolata, Convallaria majalis, Gypsophila paniculata, Fritillaria verticillata

Kranzunterlage (Oasis), Pappschachteln (Kaufhaus)

Page 70-77

Eustoma grandiflorum, Rosa cultivar, Paeonia lactiflora, Alstroemeria ligtu, Pulsatilla vulgaris, Viburnum opulus, Clematis, Alchemilla mollis, Lathyrus odoratus, Ornithogalum arabicum, Galax urceolata, Convallaria majalis, Gypsophila paniculata, Fritillaria verticillata

floral foam base (Oasis), card boxes (department store)

Seite 78–83

Xanthorrhoea australis, Zantedeschia, Xerophyllum tenax, Lilium longiflorum

Zylindrische Glasvasen (Sandra Rich); Band (Halbach); Schmuckperlen (GM-Design); Plexiglaswürfel (GM-Design)

Page 78-83

Xanthorrhoea australis, Zantedeschia, Xerophyllum tenax, Lilium longiflorum

cylindrical glass vases (Sandra Rich); ribbon (Halbach); decorative beads (GM-Design); Plexiglas cubes (GM-Design)

Seite 84–91

Narcissus incomparabilis, Tulipa, Tulipa fosteriana, Hyacinthus orientalis, Iris reticulata, Vaccinium

Glasgefäße (Klocke); Band (Halbach); Perlen, Stecknadeln (GM-Design); Draht (Buco)

Page 84-91

Narcissus incomparabilis, Tulipa, Tulipa fosteriana, Hyacinthus orientalis, Iris reticulata, Vaccinium

glass containers (Klocke); ribbon (Halbach); beads, pins (GM-Design); wire (Buco)

Seite 92–99

Rosa Cultivar, Campanula medium, Zinnia elegans, Lysimachia ephemerum, Matricaria recutita, Panicum capillare, Erysimum cheiri, Piper ornatum, Gloriosa superba,

Aristea africana, Lunaria annua, Eustoma grandiflorum, Capsella, Xanthorrhoea australis

Band (Halbach); Glasperlen (Euro-Sand); Filzblüten (Halbach); Schmucknadeln (Klocke)

Page 92-99

Rosa cultivar, Campanula medium, Zinnia elegans, Lysimachia ephemerum, Matricaria recutita, Panicum capillare, Erysimum cheiri, Piper ornatum, Gloriosa superba, Aristea africana, Lunaria anuua, Eustoma grandiflorum, Capsella, Xanthorrhoea australis

ribbon (Halbach); glass beads (Euro-Sand); felt flowers (Halbach); decorative pins (Klocke)

Seite 100–107

Salvia officinalis, Thymus pannonicus, Rosmarinus officinalis, Origanum, Dianthus caryophyllus, Dianthus plumarius, Rosa Cultivar, Olea europaea, Lavandula angustifolia, Galax urceolata

Band (Halbach); Tischläufer (Vivant); längliche Steckschaumschalen (Oasis); breites Samtband (Senn); Etageren (Schuster); Teller mit Kerze (Sia); Geschirr (Becker)

Page 100-107

Salvia officinalis, Thymus pannonicus, Rosmarinus officinalis, Origanum, Dianthus caryophyllus, Dianthus plumarius, Rosa cultivar, Olea europaea, Lavandula angustifolia, Galax urceolata

ribbon (Halbach); table runner (Vivant); long floral foam trays (Oasis); broad velvet ribbon (Senn); étagères (Schuster); plate with candle (Sia); dishes (Becker)

Seite 108–115

Gypsophila paniculata, Leucanthemum superbum, Leucanthemum vulgare, Zinnia elegans, Bouvardia, Dianthus barbatus, Allium karataviense, Nigella damascena, Stachys byzantina, Scabiosa stellata

Tischläufer, Servietten (Klocke), Teller, Kartenhalter (Ikea); runde Steckschaumunterlagen mit Drahtgitter (Oasis); Gimpe, schmales Band (Halbach); breites Band (Senn); Glasteller (Klocke)

Page 108-115

Gypsophila paniculata, Leucanthemum superbum, Leucanthemum vulgare, Zinnia elegans, Bouvardia, Dianthus barbatus, Allium karataviense, Nigella damascena, Stachys byzantina, Scabiosa stellata

table runner, serviettes (Klocke), plate, cardholder (Ikea); round floral foam base with wire mesh, (Oasis); gimp, narrow ribbon (Halbach); wide ribbon (Senn); glass plate (Klocke)

Seite 116–121

Rosa Cultivar, Gypsophila paniculata

Perlen (GM-Design); Glaspokale (Sandra Rich); goldener Deko-

Ständer (Trautz); Band (Senn), Tapetenbordüre (Baumarkt)

Page 116-121

Rosa cultivar, Gypsophila paniculata

beads (GM-Design); glass goblets (Sandra Rich); golden deco stand (Trautz); ribbon (Senn), wallpaper border (DIY Centre)

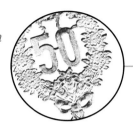

Private Feste
private parties

Seite 124–129

Calluna vulgaris, Rosa Cultivar, Dahlia, Lathyrus odoratus, Symphoricarpos albus, Chrysanthemum, Senecio bicolor

Glaspokale (Drescher); Tischläufer (Klocke); Servietten (Duni); längliche Steckschaumschalen (Oasis)

Page 124-129

Calluna vulgaris, Rosa cultivar, Dahlia, Lathyrus odoratus, Symphoricarpos albus, Chrysanthemum, Senecio bicolor

glass goblets (Drescher); table runner (Klocke); serviettes (Duni); long floral foam trays (Oasis)

Seite 130–135

Buxus sempervirens, Helianthus annuus, Rosa Cultivar, Chrysanthemum, Hypericum, Malus sylvestris

Braune Töpfe mit hellem Rand (Spang); Bänder (Halbach, Senn); Bilderrahmen (Ikea)

Page 130-135

Buxus sempervirens, Helianthus annuus, Rosa cultivar, Chrysanthemum, Hypericum, Malus sylvestris

Brown pots with light rims (Spang); ribbons (Halbach, Senn); picture frames (Ikea)

Seite 136–141

Tulipa, Narcissus, Anemone coronaria, Ranunculus asiaticus, Hyacinthus orientalis, Narcissus pseudonarcissus, Myosotis sylvatica, Aristea africana, Vaccinium, Betula pubescens, Cornus, Thymus

Zinkgefäße (Klocke); Spiegel (Ikea); Kunststoffblüten-Serviettenringe (flora center); Filzblumen, Band (Halbach)

Page 136-141

Tulipa, Narcissus, Anemone coronaria, Ranunculus asiaticus, Hyacinthus orientalis, Narcissus pseudonarcissus, Myosotis sylvatica, Aristea africana, Vaccinium, Betula pubescens, Cornus, Thymus zinc containers (Klocke); mirror (Ikea); plastic flower serviette rings (flora center); felt flowers, ribbon (Halbach)

Seite 142-147
Calluna vulgaris, Dahlia, Callistephus chinensis, Chrysanthemum, Gomphrena globosa, Rosa canina, Viburnum opulus, Ligustrum vulgare, Clematis, Hedera helix, Malus sylvestris

Vasen (Sandra Rich); Gimpe (Halbach)

Page 142-147
Calluna vulgaris, Dahlia, Callistephus chinensis, Chrysanthemum, Gomphrena globosa, Rosa canina, Viburnum opulus, Ligustrum vulgare, Clematis, Hedera helix, Malus sylvestris

vases (Sandra Rich); gimp (Halbach)

Adressen

adresses

Arte GmbH, D – 74535 Mainhardt, T +49 7903-3911, www.arte-kerzen.de

ASA Selection GmbH, D – 56203 Höhr-Grenzhausen, T +49 2624-189-0, www.asa-selection.de

Becker am Markt, D – 32423 Minden, T +49 571-83742-0, www.becker-am-markt.de

Boltze Ideen Deutschland, D – 22926 Ahrensburg, T +49 4102-4820, www.Boltze-Gruppe.de

Buco - vom Braucke GmbH & Co. KG, D – 58675 Hemer, T +49 2372-98800, www.buco-wire.com

Drescher Kunstgewerbe, D – 97525 Schwebheim, T +49 9723-2051, www.drescher-sw.de

Duni GmbH & Co. KG, D – 49565 Bramsche, T +49 5461-820, www.duni.de

Euro-Sand GmbH, D – 92637 Weiden, T +49 961-38158-0, www.eurosand.de

1.2.3 Floral Ideen / FCC GmbH, D – 99974 Mühlhausen, T +49 3601-815083, www.fcc123.de

flora center R. Tétaz AG, CH – 8412 Neftenbach, T +41 52-3050000, F +41 52-3050019, www.flora-center.de

GM-Design, D – 59557 Lippstadt, T +49 2941-3122, www.gm-design.de

Goldina Loy GmbH & Co. KG, D – 86899 Landsberg, T +49 8191-9452-0, www.goldina.de

Halbach Seidenbänder Vertrieb GmbH, D – 42899 Remscheid, T +49 2191-9583-0, www.halbach-seidenbaender.com

Hey-Sign, D – 40474 Düsseldorf, T +49 211-4543730, www.hey-sign.de

Ikea, D – 65719 Hofheim/Wallau, T +49 1805-353433, www.ikea.de

Friedrich Klocke GmbH & Co. KG, D – 32438 Porta Westfalica, T +49 571-798500, www.klocke-online.de

Metro AG, D – 40235 Düsseldorf, T +49 211-969-0, www.metrogroup.de

Molca Design AG, CH – 6023 Rothenburg, T +41 41-2808422, www.molca.com

Smithers-Oasis Germany GmbH, D – 67269 Grünstadt, T +49 6359-80040, www.smithersoasis.com

Sandra Rich GmbH, D – 56221 Ransbach-Baumbach, T +49 2623-850, www.sandrarich.de

Senn Emotion by Textiles en Biais, F – 68302 Saint-Lois Cedex, T +33 38970-2222, www.textiles-en-biais.fr

Sia Deutschland GmbH, D – 54294 Trier-Zewen, T +49 651-84044-0, www.sia-collection.de

Siegfried Schuster GmbH, D – 04509 Leipzig, T +49 341-4618141

Keramik-Spang GmbH, D – 74385 Pleidelsheim, T +49 7144-80260, www.spang-online.de

E. Trautz GmbH & Co. KG, D – 67435 Neustadt, T +49 6327-97770, www.trautz.de

Vivant, NL – 6241 JB Bunde, T +31 43-3641799, www.vivant.nl

Johannes Zemlin GmbH, D – 25469 Halstenbek, T +49 4101-599500, www.j-zemlin.com

Unser herzlicher Dank für das zur Verfügung stellen ihrer Räumlichkeiten gilt:
For the loan of rooms our sincere thanks go to:

Cafe-Bistro-Restaurant Prinz Friedrich / Minden

Hotel-Restaurant Altes Zollhaus / Rinteln

Medienzentrum u. Studios Media Dock's / Lübeck

Mexikaner im Hofviertel / Minden

Restaurant „La Tannerie", Altera Hotel / Stadthagen

Schlossküche Mövenpick in den Herrenhäuser Gärten / Hannover

Herausgeber / Publisher
FMS Floristik Marketing Service GmbH, Ratingen

Konzeption / Concept
Kerstin Theobald, Karen Meier-Ebert

Floristische Leitung / Floristic Direction
Kerstin Theobald

Floristik / Floristry
Marie-Luise Lebsanft, Petra Böttger, Guido Camin, Bettina von
Hollen, Stephan Pantze, Petra Schwörer, Kerstin Theobald

Text / Text
Karen Meier-Ebert

Redaktion / Editor
Karen Meier-Ebert, Hella Henckel

Grafische Leitung / Layout
Silvia Weichert

Grafische Gestaltung / Graphic Design
Silvia Weichert, Marion Hennig, Christine Kern

Herstellung / Production
Bettina Münch, Kabir Kapoor

Fotos / Photos
Patrick Pantze-Werbefotografie GmbH, Lage

Druck / Printing
Egedsa, Sabadell, España

Übersetzung / Translation
Janet Brümmer, Düsseldorf

© 2005 Floristik Marketing Service GmbH (FMS)
Am Potekamp 6 – 40885 Ratingen / Deutschland
Telefon: +49-2102-9644-0, Fax: +49-2102-896073
e-mail: info@fms-online.de
1. Auflage 2005

ISBN 3-9809010-7-6